Lecture Notes
in Business Information Processing

443

More information about this series at https://link.springer.com/bookseries/7911

Shaokun Fan · Noyan Ilk · Zhe Shan ·
Kexin Zhao (Eds.)

From Grand Challenges to Great Solutions

Digital Transformation in the Age of COVID-19

20th Workshop on e-Business, WeB 2021
Virtual Event, December 11, 2021
Revised Selected Papers

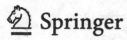

Editors
Shaokun Fan
Oregon State University
Corvallis, OR, USA

Zhe Shan (iD)
Miami University
Oxford, OH, USA

Noyan Ilk (iD)
Florida State University
Tallahassee, FL, USA

Kexin Zhao (iD)
University of North Carolina at Charlotte
Charlotte, NC, USA

ISSN 1865-1348 ISSN 1865-1356 (electronic)
Lecture Notes in Business Information Processing
ISBN 978-3-031-04125-9 ISBN 978-3-031-04126-6 (eBook)
https://doi.org/10.1007/978-3-031-04126-6

Preface

This book constitutes revised selected papers from the 20th Workshop on e-Business, WeB 2021, which took place virtually on December 11, 2021.

The Workshop on e-Business aims to provide an open forum for e-Business researchers and practitioners worldwide, to share topical research findings, explore novel ideas, discuss success stories and lessons learned, map out major challenges, and collectively chart future directions for e-Business.

The WeB 2021 theme was "From Grand Challenges to Great Solutions: Digital Transformation in the Age of COVID-19". The past decade has witnessed an unrelenting exponential growth in digital and e-Business technologies that transform how we interact, live, and work – from communication to entertainment to employment. Adoption of these technologies has never been more important than in current times. When the COVID-19 pandemic shut down the physical world, many business industries, ranging from retail, hospitality, and finance to education, were compelled to swiftly migrate into remote/digital environments in order to survive. As the world has started to slowly recover from this unprecedented event, the sustainability and the longevity of such rapid digital transformation is now a matter of debate.

The purpose of the workshop was to provide a forum for IS academics and practitioners to identify and explore the issues, opportunities, and solutions related to e-Business, digital transformation, and IT-enabled recovery in the post-pandemic era. The eight papers included in this volume were carefully reviewed and selected from a total of 24 submissions. The contributions are organized into two topical sections: 1. Digital Innovation and Transformation and 2. E-commerce and Social Media.

December 2021

Shaokun Fan
Noyan Ilk
Zhe Shan
Kexin Zhao

Organization

Honorary Chairs

Hsinchun Chen   University of Arizona, USA
Michael J. Shaw   University of Illinois at Urbana-Champaign, USA
Andrew B. Whinston   University of Texas at Austin, USA

Conference Co-chairs

Shaokun Fan   Oregon State University, USA
Noyan Ilk   Florida State University, USA
Zhe "Jay" Shan   Miami University, USA
Kexin Zhao   University of North Carolina at Charlotte, USA

Publicity Chairs

Prasanna Karhade   University of Hawai'i at Mānoa, USA
Xiao Liu   Arizona State University, USA

Advisory Committee

Kenny Cheng   University of Florida, USA
Ming Fan   University of Washington, USA
Karl Lang   City University of New York, Baruch College, USA
Jennifer Xu   Bentley University, USA
Han Zhang   Georgia Institute of Technology, USA
Bin Zhu   Oregon State University, USA

Program Committee

Hsin-lu Chang   National Chengchi University, China
Michael Chau   University of Hong Kong, China
Cheng Chen   University of Wisconsin-Milwaukee, USA
Ching-chin Chern   National Taiwan University, China
Huihui Chi   ESCP Business School, France
Su Dong   Fayetteville State University, USA
Yuheng Hu   University of Illinois at Chicago, USA

Contents

Digital Innovation and Transformation

Drivers of Technological Innovation in SMEs During Covid-19 Times: An Analysis in the Caribbean Region Using ICONOS Program Database

Danielle Nunes Pozzo[✉] [iD] and Andrea Porras-Paez [iD]

Universidad de la Costa, CUC, Barranquilla, ATL 080002, Colombia
{dnunez8,aporras2}@cuc.edu.co

Abstract. Technological innovation is still a challenge for SMEs in emerging countries, mainly due to the lack of financial, structural, capital, and proper managerial resources. Covid-19 presented a scenario that increased difficulties for companies, especially of this kind, and at the same time presented a necessity-driven impulse to look for innovative solutions. This study aimed to analyze the drivers of technological innovations of SMEs of the Caribbean Region, during what was considered locally the most critical period of covid-19 pandemic. Data was obtained from ICONOS program, a local government initiative that support the systemic development of innovations and support to consolidate organizational and regional competitive advantage. A sample of 28 innovation projects – in which 11 are already active and functional - was considered, using coding to establish the main relations and topics emerging from the different proposals. Results show covid-19 was considered both as an antecedent and as a parameter for market orientation, suggesting a rapid response from these companies when facing economic and social changes. Healthcare, education, and agriculture were found as key sectors. Potential competitive advantages were designed on three major aspects: usability, accessibility, and sustainability. The majority of the cases presented a market pull innovation flow, predominantly focusing on covid-19 related needs and consequent solutions.

Keywords: Innovation · Technological innovation · Drivers · SMEs

1 Introduction

Innovation in SMEs is still a challenge, as companies this size present a more limited access to financial and structural resources, as well as restricted personnel and low technical capabilities [11, 25]. Managers in SMEs tend to assume multiple roles, which can negatively affect their capacity to focus on strategic aspects [52]. Also, the lack of internal capacities can represent a challenge to collaboration with other firms, even when it is potentially beneficial to the SMEs [4].

These limitations are particularly affected by economic environment and the level of government support, which increases the disparity for SMEs in emerging economies,

© Springer Nature Switzerland AG 2022
S. Fan et al. (Eds.): WeB 2021, LNBIP 443, pp. 3–14, 2022.
https://doi.org/10.1007/978-3-031-04126-6_1

such as Latin American countries [7, 37]. The Covid-19 presented an additional obstacle for SMEs general management, also impacting the dynamics of innovation by changing market patterns and resources capacity worldwide [3]. Due to this environment, government support and incentives are even more critical to mitigate SMEs mortality and maintain the development of innovations [3, 10, 13].

Many countries established emergency funds and programs to support SMEs, allowing a rapid recovery in developed economies [22, 31]. In emerging countries, lack of resources as well as accumulated economic and political problems led to a limited support in many cases, including some nations that provided an almost non-existent aid for SMEs [10, 13, 20, 28].

In Colombia, national and regional governments have become allies in the efforts to maintain funding and, after the first phase of the pandemic, even expand aid to companies [10]. In a country where over 99% of companies are SMEs [15], aids of this nature are highly demanded and often not enough [36]. ICONOS Program was created to support companies develop innovations in the innovation system of the Caribbean region, more specifically the Atlantic department of Colombia [1]. This initiative concent rates the majority of financial aid granted to companies from this region during 2020 [1]. The Atlantic department is one of the most productive regions in Colombia and presents strong potential for economic development, as opposite to its low innovation rate [1, 32].

In this context, the present study intends to analyze the drivers of technological innovation of SMEs in the Caribbean Region of Colombia based on ICONOS Project database. As complementary goals, the paper intends to expand the understanding of drivers by characterizing the antecedents of innovation described by companies, characterize the innovation flow, understand the critical market orientation aspects as well as analyze the potential competitive advantages of proposals.

Technological innovations are a strategic resource to reduce SME mortality and increase its competitiveness, as well as a way to contribute to regional and national economic growth [12, 26]. Albeit representing clear benefits to emerging economies, both practical solutions and academic publications regarding the topic still present a significant gap, especially after the systemic changes caused by covid-19 [6, 13], supporting the need for studies such as this. More specific studies are even more restricted, as no other paper addressing innovation drivers in Latin American countries during covid-19 pandemic was found on the major scientific databases (Scopus, Science Direct and Web of Science).

2   Drivers of Technological Innovation in SMEs

In SMEs, technological innovation can be a result of an opportunity-seeking approach or may be driven by necessity due to limitations or urges related mainly with companies' sustainability along the years [11, 40].

Therefore, market orientation is considered an important driver of innovation in SMEs [27, 30, 46]. In Latin America, Kolbe et al. [27] found that market orientation and internal capabilities had similar impact on innovation, emphasizing the pertinence of the variable to the context of this research. The perceptions regarding demand as well as previous market study and planning, associated with a clear competitive positioning constitute factors that potentialize both the intention to innovate and performance of process and product outputs [27, 30, 42, 46].

Not only the specific market variables are critical drivers. The environment can also interfere significantly, both as antecedent and as contextual variables, affecting a variety of aspects along the innovation process [19, 34]. Factors such as macroeconomic, political, and infrastructural elements contribute to generate results regarding innovation in SMEs with a potential to cause very different outcomes, depending on their behavior [23, 38]. As a result of this dynamic, a wide distance is observed when comparing innovation drives and results in emerging and developed countries [23, 38, 44]. Although the separation between these two groups may bring important parameters for comparison, the complexity of the environment leads to the need of more in-depth and context-specific studies. Even in the Caribbean region or Colombian case analysis, discrepancies and peculiarities show that the phenomena can present different settings and variable behaviors [33, 41, 44].

Regarding antecedents and intentions, it is also relevant to observe that different innovation flows can occur and need to be explored [5, 8, 43]. Technology push innovations are a result of organizational or systemic efforts generating knowledge and information that leads to innovation, therefore originating from science and new product development [19, 35]. On the other hand, market pull innovations highlight customers demand as a guideline to develop new products and solutions, being especially relevant to SMEs, which tend to possess a more flexible structure and a more open mindset towards learning from the market [45, 46, 49, 50]. In Latin American countries, market pull innovations as a result of a 'learning by doing' approach is a common and classical finding in studies and practitioners' observations [11, 18, 21, 39].

Both types can be highly affected by government support, to the extent that strong institutional policies and investments can be considered a third flow: government-led innovations [35]. In emerging countries, innovation is being defended as a strategy to promote both organizational and national competitiveness and, although the process is long and the resources are limited, recent studies show that government-led innovation flows are highly successful [9, 34, 47, 51]. In this study, it is understood that the ACOPI initiative consists of a group formed entirely by government-led innovations [1]. Therefore, technology push and market or demand pull are being operationalized as subtypes of innovation flow in this specific context.

Government is also a classical agent of innovation systems that in government-led innovation environments incentive open innovations in opposite of traditional close processes, amplifying the learning process, the development of individual and collective capabilities and the added value of products to the region, [19, 35, 51]. Innovations resulting of open processes in local and sectoral systems are a trend to be highlighted as a result of government positioning as well as cultural and mindset changes in companies [29, 51].

In covid-19 times, government resilience and positioning towards the consequences of the pandemic were again identified as a potential incentive and support to develop innovations or as a restriction and additional obstacle [17, 34]. Financial, regulatory, and technical support were the key aspects to this specific event, as these resources allowed companies to maintain or create new projects and programs [6, 17, 24, 34, 48, 51].

3 Methodology

This is a qualitative study, conducted by using secondary data from ICONOS program. As previously mentioned, ICONOS is a local initiative that intends to support and accelerate innovation development in the Atlantic Department of Colombia [1]. The Atlantic Department concentrates the majority of the manufacturing industry of the Caribbean Region of Colombia and represents the center of factory plants and non-tourism-related service providing [32]. Also, it follows national tendencies, as around 99% of companies are SMEs [15].

ICONOS program was created to provide local companies support of different kinds, since the organizations need to partner with Research and Superior Educational Institutions to be eligible to the grant and prove the innovation is system-based, opposite to traditional internal innovation development, in order to contribute to future innovations as well and the maturement of the local innovation system [1]. The initiative is based in the lack of historical innovation applied by local companies and its previously surveyed difficulties, and the high potential of internationalization not yet fulfilled due to restrictions in international competitiveness and inadequacy to some international standards [1].

Projects were developed in the middle of the covid-19 pandemic, between march and may, 2020, which was considered the most critical time for Colombian companies that faced a high level of operational restrictions and uncertainty [14]. A total of 147 proposals were submitted, 97 were considered eligible and 51 proposals received the grant [2]. Since the grant was limited to budget resources (approximately US$ 2,6 million), suitable projects considered eligible were kept in the database with the possibility of receiving future aid [2]. Since eligible ones were reviewed as approved, they were also considered in this data analysis.

Researchers obtained full access to 38 project proposals and after discarding non-eligible and an outlier with extremely low score (close to non-eligible), 28 projects formed the final sample. Only technological innovations were considered.

Considering the template structure used by companies to develop the project and the objectives of this study, suitable chapters were selected and integrated to generate the corpus.

ATLAS.ti and NVivo were used for data processing. Coding was initially conducted considering deductive method, basing analysis on three previously determined categories: market demand perceptions (a), antecedents (b), and intended impacts on competitiveness (c). The identification mechanism considered the topics demanded on ICONOS template and properly filled by companies, which referred essentially to the previously named categories. Output categories presented on results refer to in vivo (literal) codes presented in the proposals, only integrated by slight differences in writing, however preserving the meaning.

This initial step resulted in 5393 codes for category a, 3907 for b and 8417 for c. Axial coding followed an inductive approach, resulting in the topics aggregated in adjusted categories. Code frequencies were also used as a complementary output. In order to preserve companies' identities, projects will be identified by number (e.g., P001, P002) to present findings and discussions. Extracts are reduced to preserve industrial secrets and companies' intellectual property. Due to term connections and output results, categories were rearranged in order a, c and b, as shown in the following results.

4   Results and Discussions

The first category was renamed market orientation, due to information that emerged from data (Fig. 1). Although second, third and fourth subtopics referred specific market sectors, first category was more niche-oriented, as it integrates proposals that intend to contribute with a very specific solution for a variety of sectors, including projects that are multisectoral.

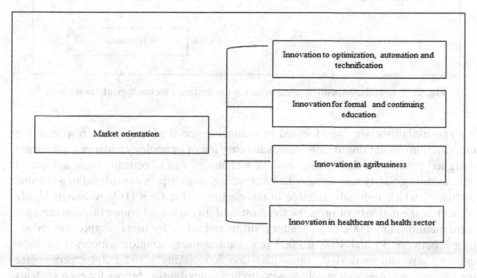

Fig. 1. Market orientation of the proposed innovations

Frequency analysis for market positioning and orientation showed a high concern with providing innovations suitable for national (0.39, Colombia) and region (0.25, Atlantic department and Caribbean) contexts. Although this can be highly affected by the type of proposal (a government grant), projects showed a high characterization of local needs and opportunities, as well as plans on how to articulate with other players in the innovation system, reinforcing the context-specific strategy. This is also supported by the fact that the proposed innovations are incremental and based on benchmarking on other markets. Service and manufacturing industry were mentioned with almost the same intensity (0.19 and 0.25, respectively) highlighting the balance of analyzed proposals.

It was also high the health concerns (0.23), even more than sector-specific market descriptions, which was expected, considering the moment the proposals were developed. However, since the grants notice did not mention or specify any covid-19 related guidelines, the high intensity of this concern in proposals is an indicative of the pandemic as a contributing factor and input to the technological innovations in the sample.

The second dimension, as presented on Fig. 2, companies' claims about the potential competitive advantages of innovation proposals focused on 3 main aspects: usability, accessibility, and sustainability.

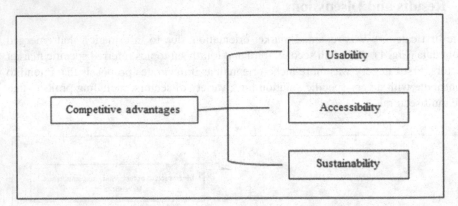

Fig. 2. Potential competitive advantages for the designed technological innovations

The usability claim was focused in enhancing speed of access and response, the introduction of solutions to autonomous and easy use of technology and user-customized designed products. Additionally, intuitive technology was a recurring topic associated with usability. Safety and security features were also an aspect considered to add value for users, which is highly suitable to the context at the time [16]. Although highly present in the majority of projects, the most usability-oriented competitive advantages were mentioned by P002 (e.g., "better comfort and safety for users…expects to reduce time…between 30 and 40%"), P003 (e.g. "autonomous solution supported by solar energy…any mobile device…immediate decision-making") and P008 ("personalize the experience…user to control courses' rhythm…flexibility…proper for each students learning style").

For accessibility claims, the focus were innovative payment methods, highly oriented to client needs in covid-19 context which is coherent with local financial trends and circulation restrictions at the time [16]. Accessibility was also linked as a way not only to obtain, but to maintain clients, as accessible products and processes could lead to a higher value perception and consequent customer loyalty (as in P004: "a solution…differentiates…alternative and integrated payment directly on platform…incorporate long-term relationships" and in P009 "if restricted to only electronic payment, many people would not…to pay electronically", showing inclusion concerns).

Sustainability was a topic of high intensity in all 28 projects. Safety and security are again present as connected to this topic, as a way of providing more lasting solutions. Both internal and external efficiency and smart use of resources were relevant in sustainable-oriented claims. Another perspective of this subtopic worthy of highlighting is the connectivity and capacity to integrate with other systems and platforms, giving the economic pillar of sustainability a strong connection with usability. Some evidences support this subtopic, can be exemplified by P005 ("reduce up to 80% of water usage...reduce the use of land...decrease energy costs for food storage and transportation"), P006 ("inputs from all platforms...reducing risk of fraud..."), P009 ("there is no hybrid...system in Colombia") and P010 ("the integration of the platform is another element that differentiates this platform from the similar tools currently available").

In terms of frequency analysis, the awareness of the need to provide clear benefits for users and consumers were represented by a variety of codes along the projects (0.62). Alternatives were mentioned in terms to enhance customer experience, provide rewards, and include processes of gamification. Service coverage (0.27) was also a critical topic and also a justification to implement innovations. Such results provide a suitable complementary view to the aforementioned subtopics.

Finally, in antecedents' analysis, the frequency replicates the concern about service coverage, previously mentioned in competitive claims, showing the lack of coverage as a reason to apply technological innovation (0.32). This evidence highlights the tendency to establish a previous market research to support technological innovations and to connect those results to potential competitive advantages, a link that, although critical, is not always present on SMEs innovations [52]. Health and safety concerns were also high (0.29), showing not only the intent to contribute to and consider a pandemic environment as a market variable but also that this aspect was already perceived as a critical matter in the beginning of march, 2020, when the concept of these innovations was created.

In order to understand innovation flow, antecedent codes were processed to observe the intensity of 'market pull' and 'technology push' approaches, resulting in a concentration of 67,85% and 32,15%, respectively. According to data, this predominance of market demands is highly connected with economic and social consequences of the pandemic outbreak as well as customers' needs, indicating that companies were more likely to invest in projects to support immediate and necessary solutions. This is also supported by the fact that all analyzed projects proposed a 1-to-2-year schedule to implement final innovations. Table 1 presents the subcategories of innovation flow.

Table 1. Innovation flow and main purposes based on antecedents

Innovation flow	Subcategories	Frequency
Market pull	1° Innovate to preserve life and health	60%
	2° Innovate to maintain education, professional training, and skill improvement	20%
	3° Innovate to provide security and reduce opportunistic behavior on the market	11%
	4° Innovate to enhance regional and national productivity and competitivity	9%
Technology push	1° Innovate to improve process performance, perceived quality and efficiency	78%
	2° Innovate to contribute to company's sustainability on the market	22%

Results reinforce the relevance of covid-19 pandemic and its consequences as an antecedent to innovate. Considering this as a pillar of innovation development, it provides strong evidence of its impact on local innovation system and the rapid response of the sample companies in terms of adaptation, market analysis and new product development, replicating results found by Adam and Alarifi [3] in Saudi Arabia and [13] in Mexico. Considering the strict measures to reduce circulation applied by local government [16] and the continuous need for specialized professionals, the second subcategory is understood as highly connected with the first one, as a way to mitigate and contribute to current market changes. The increased usage of technology to reduce circulation and its consequent increased security risk in everyday life is also a strong consequence of covid-19 outbreak in the Caribbean region [16], which can also support the connection of this market demand to the pandemic context.

Furthermore, although subcategories relate with previous market orientation and competitive advantages, environmental and social impacts were not identified as antecedents in technology push innovations. This may lead to the understanding that, when addressing technology push innovations, companies were more inclined to think about its direct relation with customers and traditional performance results (e.g., profit, sales volume, etc.), opening an enquiry for future research.

5   Conclusions and Future Directions

This research intended to contribute to current literature regarding technological innovation in SMEs, more specifically in emerging economies by focusing on drivers extracted from projects approved in ICONOS program, an initiative based on the Caribbean region of Colombia.

Although proposals were developed at the beginning of covid-19 pandemic, the outbreak and its consequences were already considered as both antecedent and a competitive factor for innovation implementation. Although this may not seem surprising as a conclusion, Colombian companies are traditionally characterized as slow in terms of responding to adversity [15, 51]. Results indicates a fast response from the analyzed companies, which could suggest that, although innovation levels are historically low, covid-19 could relevantly change local companies' behavior towards innovation. Since 2020 was the first year of ICONOS, this limit direct comparisons, however future studies can map other grant notices offered by local government along the years. Sustainability and accessibility concerns as critical variables of technological innovation development are also a contextual highlight that could indicate a market trend, due to its discrepancy if compared to previous (and limited) studies [15, 51].

A relevant limitation of this study, besides the database per se, is that, although many players are part of the regional innovation system, the institutional education supporting all the analyzed proposals was the same, which can lead to some level of bias. Considering all of the projects were considered suitable and eligible by the government, it is a fair assumption that it represents valid justification and proper representation of the concerns and analysis of the context. However, a further look into other universities' proposals is needed for confirmation and potentially, identification of nuances that are not visible from this perspective.

A study considering all eligible proposals in a longitudinal analysis could lead to deep and more representative results of the Atlantic Department. A comparison between Colombia regions as well as Latin America and Caribbean countries would also be a very interesting addition to the current literature and could help understand the intricacies and specificities of regionals and nationals' innovation systems.

It is also pertinent to include additional data to expand the comprehension of drivers and its dynamics (including interviews, observation, and other sources of data) as well as cross and possibly validate the first discussions presented on this paper. Additionally, it is expected that the robustness of multiple sources and cross-data analysis may lead to the proposal of a theoretical framework derived of the studied phenomenon.

Regarding innovation flow, it is proper to remark that only technology push and market pull approaches were considered, not including design-driven flow as a third category [49]. Although suitable to the study, the nature and volume of data did not allow a clear separation between the classical technology push type and the more recent definition of design-driven, since the results of innovation process (innovation products) were not entirely available at the time. This is also a possible path for future studies.

Even though it is not the focus of this paper, it is relevant to highlight that out of the 28 eligible projects analyzed, 11 were granted and all innovations were implemented before September 2021, reinforcing the suitability of the projects and supporting the effectiveness of this local government incentive. Therefore, it is a relevant phenomenon to be taking into consideration. An analysis of ICONOS case from complementary perspectives is already in course as it is understood that these successful results can be an important reference for replication in different but yet similar, environments.

References

1. ACOPI: Realización de la fase de cofinanciación en el marco del proyecto; implementación de un programa de cofinanciación de proyectos de I+D+I en pymes de sectores estratégicos en el departamento del Atlántico. http://iconosatlantico.com/wp-content/uploads/2020/03/TDR-DEFINITIVOS-ICONOS-02.03.20.pdf. Accessed 10 Aug 2020
2. ACOPI: Publicación de resultados definitivos de la evaluación técnica. http://iconosatlantico.com/wp-content/uploads/2020/06/LISTADO-DEFINITIVO-DE-ELEGIBLES-EVALTEC-1.pdf. Accessed 10 Aug 2020
3. Adam, N.A., Alarifi, G.: Innovation practices for survival of small and medium enterprises (SMEs) in the COVID-19 times: the role of external support. J. Innov. Entrepreneurship 10(1), 1–22 (2021). https://doi.org/10.1186/s13731-021-00156-6
4. Akinremi, T., Roper, S.: The collaboration paradox: why small firms fail to collaborate for innovation. In: Fernandes, G., Dooley, L., O'Sullivan, D., Rolstadås, A. (eds.) Managing Collaborative R&D Projects, pp. 139–159. Springer, Cham (2021). https://doi.org/10.1007/978-3-030-61605-2_8
5. Amalia, N.V., Sutopo, W., Hisjam, M.: Technopreneurship & innovation system: a comparative analysis for batik wastewater treatment equipment technology development in Indonesia. In: 3rd International Conference on Engineering and Information Technology for Sustainable Industry (ICONETSI), pp.1–6. ACM International Conference Proceeding Series, Indonesia (2020). https://doi.org/10.1145/3429789.3429863
6. Amuda, Y.J.: Impact of coronavirus on small and medium enterprises (SMEs): towards post-covid-19 economic recovery in Nigeria. Acad. Strateg. Manag. J. 19(6), 1–11 (2020)

7. Arza, V., López, E.: Obstacles affecting innovation in small and medium enterprises: quantitative analysis of the Argentinean manufacturing sector. Res. Policy **50**(9), 1–19 (2021). https://doi.org/10.1016/j.respol.2021.104324
8. Babalola, O.O., Amiolemen, S.O., Adegbite, S.A., Ojo-Emmanuel, G.: Evaluation of factors influencing technological innovations of small and medium enterprises in Nigerian industrial estates. Int. J. Innov. Sci. **7**(1), 39–53 (2015). https://doi.org/10.1260/1757-2223.7.1.39
9. Beltramino, N.S., García-Perez-de-Lema, D., Valdez-Juárez, L.E.: The structural capital, the innovation and the performance of the industrial SMES. J. Intellect. Cap. **21**(6), 913–945 (2020). https://doi.org/10.1108/JIC-01-2019-0020
10. BID: Instrumentos de financiamiento para las micro, pequeñas y medianas empresas en América Latina y el Caribe durante el Covid-19. https://publications.iadb.org/publications/spanish/document/Instrumentos-de-financiamiento-para-las-micro-pequenas-y-medianas-empresas-en-America-Latina-y-el-Caribe-durante-el-Covid-19.pdf. Accessed 20 Sept 2021
11. Bitencourt, C.C., de Oliveira Santini, F., Zanandrea, G., Froehlich, C., Ladeira, W.J.: Empirical generalizations in eco-innovation: a meta-analytic approach. J. Clean. Prod. **245**, 1–26 (2020). https://doi.org/10.1016/j.jclepro.2019.118721
12. Branscomb, L.M.: Technological innovation. In: Smelser, N.J., Baltes, P.B. (eds.) International Encyclopedia of the Social & Behavioral Sciences, Pergamon, New York (2001). https://doi.org/10.1016/B0-08-043076-7/03208-3
13. Caballero-Morales, S.: Innovation as recovery strategy for SMEs in emerging economies during the COVID-19 pandemic. Res. Int. Bus. Financ. **57**, 1–9 (2021). https://doi.org/10.1016/j.ribaf.2021.101396
14. CEPAL: Compilación de estadísticas de cuentas nacionales, balanza de pagos y comercio exterior en el marco de la emergencia sanitaria de la enfermedad por coronavirus (COVID-19). https://www.cepal.org/es/publicaciones/45666-compilacion-estadisticas-cuentas-nacionales-balanza-pagos-comercio-exterior. Accessed 16 Sept 2021
15. CEPAL: Mipymes en América Latina: un frágil desempeño y nuevos desafíos para las políticas de foment. https://www.cepal.org/es/publicaciones/44148-mipymes-america-latina-un-fragil-desempeno-nuevos-desafios-politicas-fomento. Accessed 16 Sept 2021
16. CEPAL: Sectors and businesses facing COVID-19: emergency and reactivation. https://repositorio.cepal.org/bitstream/handle/11362/45736/5/S2000437_en.pdf. Accessed 16 Sept 2021
17. Chatterjee, S., Chaudhuri, R.: Supply chain sustainability during turbulent environment: examining the role of firm capabilities and government regulation. Oper. Manag. Res., 1–15 (2021). https://doi.org/10.1007/s12063-021-00203-1
18. Fernández, S., Torrecillas, C., Labra, R.E.: Drivers of eco-innovation in developing countries: the case of Chilean firms. Technol. Forecast. Soc. Change **170**, 1–18 (2021). https://doi.org/10.1016/j.techfore.2021.120902
19. Ferreira, J.J.M., Teixeira, S.J., Rammal, H.G.: Technological Innovation and International Competitiveness for Business Growth: Challenges and Opportunities, 1st edn. Palgrave Macmillan, London (2021)
20. Ganlin, P., Qamruzzaman, M.D., Mehta, A.M., Naqvi, F.N., Karim, S.: Innovative finance, technological adaptation and SMEs sustainability: the mediating role of government support during covid-19 pandemic. Sustainability (Switzerland) **13**(16), 1–27 (2021). https://doi.org/10.3390/su13169218
21. García Ortiz, P.A., Calderón García, H., Fayos Gardó, T., Roa Vivas, N.: Dynamic marketing capabilities as drivers of international channel integration: is this true for Latin American SMEs? Qual. Market Res. **24**(5), 653–682 (2021). https://doi.org/10.1108/QMR-01-2021-0007
22. Groenewegen, J., Hardeman, S., Stam, E.: Does COVID-19 state aid reach the right firms? COVID-19 state aid, turnover expectations, uncertainty and management practices. J. Bus. Ventur. Insights **16**, 1–8 (2021). https://doi.org/10.1016/j.jbvi.2021.e00262

23. Hervas-Oliver, J., Parrilli, M.D., Sempere-Ripoll, F.: SME modes of innovation in European catching-up countries: the impact of STI and DUI drivers on technological innovation. Technol. Forecast. Soc. Change **173**, 1–11 (2021). https://doi.org/10.1016/j.techfore.2021. 121167.
24. Islam, A., Galinato, G.I., Zhang, W.: Can government spending boost firm sales? Kyklos **74**(4), 1–24 (2021). https://doi.org/10.1111/kykl.12278
25. Kapler, M.: Barriers to the implementation of innovations in information systems in SMEs. Prod. Eng. Arch. **27**(2), 156–162 (2021). https://doi.org/10.30657/pea.2021.27.20
26. Krammer, M.S.S.: Science, technology, and innovation for economic competitiveness: the role of smart specialization in less developed countries. Technol. Forecast. Soc. Chang. **123**, 95–107 (2017)
27. Kolbe, D., Frasquet, M., Calderon, H.: The role of market orientation and innovation capability in export performance of small- and medium-sized enterprises: a Latin American perspective. Multinational Bus. Rev. (2021). Ahead-of-print. https://doi.org/10.1108/MBR-10-2020-0202
28. KPMG: Embedding resilience: Addressing the business challenges presented by the coronavirus. https://home.kpmg/xx/en/home/insights/2020/03/the-business-implications-of-coronavirus.html. Accessed 20 Sept 2021
29. Lopes, J., Oliveira, M., Silveira, P., Farinha, L., Oliveira, J.: Business dynamism and innovation capacity, an entrepreneurship worldwide perspective. J. Open Innov. Technol. Market Complex. **7**(1), 1–18 (2021). https://doi.org/10.3390/JOITMC7010094
30. Madrid-Guijarro, A., Martin, D.P., García-Pérez-de-Lema, D.: Capacity of open innovation activities in fostering product and process innovation in manufacturing SMEs. RMS **15**(7), 2137–2164 (2021). https://doi.org/10.1007/s11846-020-00419-8
31. Marino, A., Pariso, P.: The global macroeconomic impacts of covid-19: four European scenarios. Acad. Strateg. Manag. J. **20**(2), 1–21 (2021)
32. MinCit, Información: Perfiles Económicos Departamentales. https://www.mincit.gov.co/get attachment/fdd96c98-45d2-451f-86c6-d200a1da9427/Perfiles-Economicos-por-Departame ntos. Accessed 16 Sept 2021
33. Morisson, A., Doussineau, M.: Regional innovation governance and place-based policies: design, implementation and implications. Reg. Stud. Reg. Sci. **6**(1), 101–116 (2019). https://doi.org/10.1080/21681376.2019.1578257
34. Najib, M., Rahman, A.A.A., Fahma, F.: Business survival of small and medium-sized restaurants through a crisis: the role of government support and innovation. Sustainability (Switzerland) **13**(19), 1–16 (2021). https://doi.org/10.3390/su131910535
35. Nemet, G.F.: Demand-pull, technology-push, and government-led incentives for non-incremental technical change. Res. Policy **38**(5), 700–709 (2009). https://doi.org/10.1016/j.respol.2009.01.004
36. OECD: Financing SMEs and Entrepreneurs 2020: An OECD Scoreboard. https://www.oecd-ilibrary.org/sites/2960938f-en/index.html?itemId=/content/component/2960938f-en. Accessed 22 Sept 2021
37. Pertuz, V., Miranda, L.F.: Perceptions of barriers to innovate in Colombian manufacturing firms: an analysis by technological intensity. Competitiveness Rev. (2021). Ahead of print. https://doi.org/10.1108/CR-08-2020-0102
38. Plechero, M., Chaminade, C.: The role of regional sectoral specialisation on the geography of innovation networks: a comparison between firms located in regions in developed and emerging economies. Int. J. Technol. Learn. Innov. Dev. **8**(2), 148–171 (2016). https://doi.org/10.1504/IJTLID.2016.077106
39. Pisicchio, A.C., Toaldo, A.M.M.: Integrated marketing communication in hospitality SMEs: analyzing the antecedent role of innovation orientation and the effect on market performance. J. Mark. Commun. **27**(7), 742–761 (2021). https://doi.org/10.1080/13527266.2020.1759121

40. Rasca, L., Deaconu, A., True, S.: From successful SMEs to entrepreneurial society and the importance of the entrepreneurial mindset. In: Suder, G., Lindeque, J. (eds.) Doing Business in Europe, 3rd edn., pp. 315–328. Sage Publications, London (2018). https://doi.org/10.1007/978-3-319-72239-9_15

41. Rodríguez, F.M., Pérez, M.V.: Bogota-region in the OECD scenario. Prisms and innovation indicators. [Bogotá-región en el escenario OCDE. Prismas e indicadores de innovación] Cuadernos De Economia (Colombia) **39**(79) 103–138 (2020). https://doi.org/10.15446/cuad.econ.v39n79.75783

42. Sáez-Martínez, F.J., Díaz-García, C., Gonzalez-Moreno, A.: Firm technological trajectory as a driver of eco-innovation in young small and medium-sized enterprises. J. Clean. Prod. **138**, 28–37 (2016). https://doi.org/10.1016/j.jclepro.2016.04.108

43. Shkabatur, J., Bar-El, R., Schwartz, D.: Innovation and entrepreneurship for sustainable development: lessons from Ethiopia. Progress Plan. (2021, article in press). https://doi.org/10.1016/j.progress.2021.100599

44. Salazar-Araujo, E.J., Pozzo, D., Cazallo-Antunez, A.M.: Innovation capacity vs. internationalization capacity: the case of Colombian manufacturing SMEs of the Atlantic region. In: 15th Iberian Conference on Information Systems and Technologies (CISTI), pp. 1–6. Iberian Association for Information Systems and Technologies, Portugal (2020). https://doi.org/10.23919/CISTI49556.2020.9141016

45. Scaringella, L., Miles, R.E., Truong, Y.: Customers involvement and firm absorptive capacity in radical innovation: the case of technological spin-offs. Technol. Forecast. Soc. Chang. **120**, 144–162 (2017). https://doi.org/10.1016/j.techfore.2017.01.005

46. Soto-Acosta, P., Popa, S., Martinez-Conesa, I.: Information technology, knowledge management and environmental dynamism as drivers of innovation ambidexterity: a study in SMEs. J. Knowl. Manag. **22**(4), 824–849 (2018). https://doi.org/10.1108/JKM-10-2017-0448

47. Spuldaro, J.D., Prim, A.L., Bencke, F.F., Roman, D.J.: The effect of innovation on the financial performance and export intensity of firms in emerging countries. Int. J. Bus. Innov. Res. **25**(3), 304–327 (2021). https://doi.org/10.1504/IJBIR.2021.116382

48. Varón Sandoval, A., González Calixto, M.B., Ramírez Salazar, M.P.: Colombia: innovation, trust and emotions during the COVID-19 pandemic. Manag. Res. **19**(1), 1–21 (2020). https://doi.org/10.1108/MRJIAM-05-2020-1040

49. Verganti, R.: Design Driven Innovation: Changing the Rules of Competition by Radically Innovating What Things Mean, 1st edn. Harvard Business Press, New York (2009)

50. Vorkapić, M., Radovanović, F., Ćoćkalo, D., Đorđević, D.: NPD in small manufacturing enterprises in Serbia. [NPD u malim proizvodnim poduzećima u Srbiji] Tehnicki Vjesnik **24**(1), 327–332 (2017). https://doi.org/10.17559/TV-20150807185156

51. Zapata-cantu, L., González, F.: Challenges for innovation and sustainable development in Latin America: the significance of institutions and human capital. Sustainability (Switzerland) **13**(7), 1–21 (2021). https://doi.org/10.3390/su13074077

52. Wang, C., Walker, E.A., Redmond, J.L.: Explaining the lack of strategic planning in SMEs: the importance of owner motivation. Int. J. Organisational Behav. **12**(1), 1–16 (2007)

Benefits of Business Intelligence Systems and Multiple National Cultures During Covid-19

Ankur Jaiswal[1]([✉]) [iD], Abhishek Kathuria[1] [iD], and Prasanna P. Karhade[2] [iD]

[1] Indian School of Business, Gachibowli, Hyderabad 500 111, Telangana, India
ankur_jaiswal@isb.edu
[2] University of Hawai'i at Mānoa, 2404 Maile Way, Honolulu, HI 96822, USA

Abstract. Infobesity presents a challenge in the information age, necessitating business intelligence systems for conducting business. The information age is also characterized by organizations spread across culturally different countries, which gain performance benefits from multiple national cultures. We study the effect of Business Intelligence Systems and Multiple National Cultures within the context of the Covid-19 pandemic that resulted in the erosion of market value of firms. We propose that though firms that used Business Intelligence Systems or benefitted from Multiple National Cultures exhibited better performance, the concurrent occurrence of these two phenomena resulted in a weakened effect on performance. Our econometric analysis of Fortune 500 firms finds strong support for our theory. We make significant contributions to the e-Business literature within the information systems discipline and to broader inter-disciplinary management research.

Keywords: Covid-19 · Business Intelligence · National Culture · Market value

1 Introduction

The information age poses several challenges to firms due to the overabundance of information – termed infobesity. Hence, information technologies (IT), such as *business intelligence systems* and their constituent data storage systems, which together are used to *store, process, and derive insights from knowledge* [1, 2], are essential for conducting both analogue and electronic business. The information age is also characterized by the rise of organizations that are *spread across culturally different countries across the globe*. As each country possesses its own unique national culture, organizations encompass multiple diverse cultures by their presence in multiple countries. Research shows that firms with *Multiple National Cultures* can leverage IT to harness diverse information across the organization for performance benefits such as insights and innovation [3].

In the recent past, business practice witnessed an abrupt disruption due to the Covid-19 pandemic. The start of the pandemic subjected organizations to large-scale, abrupt, and unexpected demand and supply shocks, resulting in erosion of market value. It is this context within which we study the effect of *Business Intelligence Systems* and *Multiple*

S. Fan et al. (Eds.): WeB 2021, LNBIP 443, pp. 15–29, 2022.
https://doi.org/10.1007/978-3-031-04126-6_2

National Cultures. Our primary thesis is that *firms that used Business Intelligence Systems or benefitted from Multiple National Cultures exhibited better performance during the Covid-19 pandemic. However, the concurrent occurrence of these two phenomena weakens the effect of one on the other on firm performance.*

Our reasoning behind this thesis is as follows. *Business Intelligence Systems* used to store, process, and derive insights from knowledge [4, 5] allowed firms to develop new ways of doing business that were necessary during the Covid-19 pandemic. Firms with *Multiple National Cultures* attained similar benefits from their diverse and distributed base of cultural knowledge [3, 6], which was also used to develop new ways of doing business. However, since both *Business Intelligence Systems* and *Multiple National Cultures* endow firms with overabundant and redundant information, organizations are unable to take quick and effective decisions as they struggle with infobesity.

We empirically test our theory by examining the stock market performance of U.S. headquartered Fortune 500 firms during the first quarter of 2020. We choose this empirical setting and specification to ensure that the health and economic effects of Covid-19 are not conflated, and our dependent variable reflects the anticipated future value of the firm while discounting past decisions [7]. Our analysis finds strong and conclusive evidence to support our thesis.

2   Related Literature

Increase in globalization over the past few decades has resulted in complex supply chains and firm operations. Organizations have sought to source from suppliers and serve customers across multiple markets located in different countries, requiring firms to maintain a simultaneous presence across multiple countries. As cultures differ across national boundaries, organizations that operate across countries possesses different cultures. The presence of firms in other countries is in the form of temporally or geographically distant employees, who are situated within the cultural environment of their host nation. Prior research has shown that globally distributed employees embody multiple cultures – a concept that has been used extensively in prior information systems research [3].

Hofstede's [8] conceptualization of national culture is the best established and has been used extensively in prior works [2, 9, 10]. Firms that operate across multiple national cultures reflect the cultural differences between countries across the dimensions of power distance, individualism, uncertainty avoidance, and masculinity [11, 12]. Greater differences in these values between countries imply higher diversity of culture [13], and thus higher *Multiple National Cultures*.

The international business, strategy, and operations management literatures have highlighted several disadvantages of operating across multiple countries for firms. These include institutional differences [14], tax regime differences, political differences, geographical distances, and most critically, cultural differences [15]. Several papers in the information systems area have focused upon these risks and/or the role that IT can play in mitigating their deleterious effects [9, 16–18].

This stream of research has shown IT and IT-enabled capabilities help firms overcome internationalization risk and compete globally [18]. IT also helps organizations that are culturally diverse and geographically dispersed globally to achieve greater innovation

[3]. However, the use of these technologies also exposes the firm to an abundance of information, which may prove deleterious under situations that require quick and efficient decision making [19].

Organizations are information processing systems and where the imbalance between the firms' information processing capabilities and the information load encountered can create information overload or underload [20]. Infobesity is a condition characterized by information overload whereby firms and decision makers collect more information than they need or more information than they can efficiently use. The increasing use of different types of information systems - such as enterprise systems, email systems – has been associated with infobesity [4, 21]. Prior studies have researched the antecedents and consequences of infobesity [22–24]. Infobesity can create stress and frustration among decision makers [22] and can have detrimental effects on organizations' success. Infobesity affects attention capacity and the ability to take decisions, thereby harming productivity, learning, and ultimately firm performance [22, 25].

As organizations across industries face infobesity, they attempt to find means to cope with it. Recent studies have begun to explain how firms perform in the presence of infobesity [4]. Whereas IT has shown to be an antecedent to infobesity, it has also been shown to a firm to transform excess information into business insights [5, 26] and thus, creating value under infobesity [27–30]. For example, IT-enabled capabilities related to information storage, management, processing, and analysis, analytical capacity, and business intelligence solutions have a positive impact on performance [2, 5, 6, 24, 31–43].

3   Theoretical Development

The initial shock from the Covid-19 pandemic necessitated firms to sense and respond to severe economic disruptions through efficient and effective decision making at speed [40, 44, 45]. Prior research in information systems has investigated the role of various incentive-based theories, such as transaction cost economics, in enhancing efficiencies of firms and their supply chains in responding to such disruptions [46, 47]. In contrast, we use the *Knowledge Based View* to articulate theoretical explanations for the performance of firms that use *Business Intelligence Systems* or incorporate *Multiple National Cultures* during the Covid-19 pandemic [46].

First, *Business Intelligence Systems (BIS)*, which include related information technologies, such as data storage systems, which are used to store, process, and derive insights from knowledge [2, 4, 5], offer opportunities to uncover new knowledge and derive combinatorial advantages from knowledge. Use of *business intelligence systems* allows firms to uncover obscure and weak signals of knowledge, which can result in exploratory innovations [2, 3, 38, 48]. New combinations of knowledge also provide firms with new ways of doing business that may be beneficial during the Covid-19 pandemic. In line, with these arguments, we posit our first hypothesis:

Hypothesis 1: Firms with Business Intelligence Systems exhibit superior firm performance during the Covid-19 pandemic.

Second, *Multiple National Cultures* within a firm can offer opportunities for applying knowledge across contexts [16]. Knowledge of cultural practices and norms provides firms opportunities to explore and exploit variance across countries and thus arbitrage economic and knowledge differences across countries [49, 50]. These opportunities may be leveraged to create new ways of doing business during the Covid-19 pandemic. Second, firms with *Multiple National Cultures* benefit from learning opportunities across dissimilar cultures with unique competencies and perspectives [6, 51, 52]. Potential combinations of these competencies and perspectives can result in an abundant and wide span of ideas, viewpoints, and practices that can be generalized across new contexts arising during the Covid-19 pandemic [53, 54]. In line, with these arguments, we posit our second hypothesis:

Hypothesis 2: Firms with Multiple National Cultures exhibit superior firm performance during the Covid-19 pandemic.

Recent research has also shown that IT can cause organizations to suffer from information overload or *infobesity* [4, 36–38, 55]. Infobesity is a *condition characterized by information overload whereby firms collect more information than they need or more information than they can efficiently use, which can overwhelm the processing capabilities of an organization and its decision makers* [56]. The presence of *Multiple National Cultures* also increases the combinatorial complexity and redundancy of information and thus infobesity within the firm [40]. Furthermore, uncovering new knowledge patterns, arbitrage opportunities, and combinatorial advantages requires time to analyze, compare, and evaluate different options – a scare resource during extreme shocks. These arguments lead us to our third hypothesis:

Hypothesis 3: The concurrent presence of Business Intelligence Systems and Multiple National Cultures has a negative effect on firm performance during the Covid-19 pandemic.

4 Methods

4.1 Methodology

Our research theorizes that firms which receive abnormal rewards during the Covid-19 pandemic, have superior *Business Intelligence Systems* and *Multiple National Cultures*. Though there has been ample work using accounting-based measures of performance in prior information systems literature [19, 43, 57–60], however these are not suitable for our current research design. Therefore, we utilize an event study methodology to estimate the abnormal returns which are associated with specific events, after controlling for the market-wide factors which influence stock prices [61]. This methodology relies on the assumptions of the efficient market hypothesis, which postulates that capital markets reflect all the information that occur quickly and accurately in determining security prices.

In our study, we examine the Covid-19 event [62, 63], by estimating the stock market performance at the onset of the quarter in the year 2020. We translate the calendar days into event days, such that Day 0 is the event day when the market started to decline, Day 1, 2 and so on are the trading days following the event day, while Day −1, −2 and so on are the trading days before the event day. We assume the return generating process that the asset follows is the market model [64, 65]. The market model assumes that stock return and market return are related over a given period through the relationship specified below in Eq. (1):

$$R_{it} = \alpha_i + \beta_i R_{mt} + \varepsilon_{it} \tag{1}$$

where R_{it} is the return of stock i in time t, R_{mt} is the market return in time t, and α_i is the intercept of the relationship for stock i. β_i is the systematic risk (or beta) of stock i, which captures the sensitivity of stock i's return to the market return. ε_{it} is the error term for stock i in time t.

The movement of stock i's return that is attributed to the market movement is represented by $\beta_i R_{mt}$ (the systematic component of stock i return) and ε_{it} (the idiosyncratic component of stock i return) represents the portion of the return for stock i that is unexplained by market movements. The S&P 500 index is used as the benchmark for the market return. We use ordinary least squares regression over a period of 2017 to 2019 to estimate $\widehat{\alpha}_i$ and $\widehat{\beta}_i$ for each stock i and consequently estimate the Abnormal Return for the first quarter of 2020.

Thereafter, we employ a cross-section regression specification for our analysis to assess our hypothesized model. The cross-sectional regression of Firm Performance is as specified in Eq. (2) below:

$$Firm\,Performance_i = \beta_0 + \beta_1 BIS + \beta_2 MNC_i + \beta_3 MNC_i * BIS_i + \beta_4 X_i + \beta_5 \varphi_i + \epsilon_i \tag{2}$$

The unit of observation is firm i during the first quarter of 2020. *Business Intelligence Systems (BIS)* and *Multiple National Cultures (MNC)* are the variables of interest, which are measured with a lag of one year for each firm i, at the end of year 2018. The coefficient β_1 captures the direct effect of *Business Intelligence Systems* of firm i on its *Firm Performance*, the coefficient β_2 captures the direct effect of *Multiple National Cultures* of firm i on its *Firm Performance*, and β_3 is the parameter that captures the interaction effect of *Business Intelligence Systems* and *Multiple National Cultures* of firm i on its *Firm Performance*, during the first quarter of 2020. X_i controls for time variant firm-level variables for firm i, measured at the end of quarter in 2019 and φ controls for industry effects based on the *Fama–French* industry group for firm i. A key strength of this regression specification is that it is not associated with a specific shock date.

4.2 Data

We combine data from five archival sources to create a unique dataset for Fortune 500 firms. We obtain the locations of each firm's major subsidiaries from a proprietary database [3, 5, 6, 54]. We obtain the Hofstede cultural dimensions scores from Geert Hofstede's webpage. Prior studies have extensively used such data of location of subsidiaries and culture e.g., [2, 66]. This location data together with Hofstede cultural dimensions scores is used to create the independent variable *Multiple National Cultures* of our study.

We estimate a firm's *Business Intelligence Systems* from the Computer Intelligence (CI) Technology Database of Harte-Hanks Market Intelligence. The CI database, formerly the Harte-Hanks database, has been widely used in prior research on the impacts of IT [67–70]. We obtain data on stock returns from the Center for Research in Security Prices database. Data from the first quarter of 2020 is utilized to create the dependent variable of our study and data on stock returns for all quarters of 2017 to 2019 is used in the market model to estimate abnormal market returns. Finally, we retrieve quarterly accounting data for quarter four of 2019 from the WRDS - North America Compustat, Fundamentals Quarterly. This company and accounting information data is used to create the array of control variables for our regression specifications. After matching all datasets, our final sample consists of observations for 363 distinct firms.

4.3 Variables

Independent Variables. Our primary independent variable is the firm's *Business Intelligence Systems*, which is constructed from the CI database. The CI database provides information on implementation of various digital technologies across different sites of a firm. For our analysis, we aggregate site-level data to the firm-level. Consistent with prior literature [1, 2, 35, 38, 43, 71], the measure of *Business Intelligence Systems* constitutes the summative score of business intelligence and data storage digital technologies possessed by the firm at the end of 2018.

Our second independent variable encapsulates the diverse national cultures subsumed within a firm by virtue of its geographical spread and presence in culturally different countries across the globe [2, 9, 18, 72]. As described in the theory development section, the employees of the subsidiaries of these firms, which have a global presence, embody the knowledge and attributes of the national cultures of countries in which they reside and operate. Therefore, conjoint with the location of the firms' subsidiaries and Hofstede's cultural dimensions scores, we measure *Multiple National Cultures*. This research design is aligned with prior literature which notes that subsidiaries "reflect the values, norms, and locally accepted practices of the societies in which they operate" ([73], p. 345).

Primarily *Multiple National Cultures* uses the well-established measure of cultural distance [74, 75] for each subsidiary pair [13], which is based on deviation of the two countries along four of Hofstede's cultural dimensions (i.e., power distance, individualism, masculinity, uncertainty avoidance, [76]). Thereafter the measure of *Multiple National Cultures* for a firm is arrived by taking an average of cultural distances for all possible pairs of subsidiaries of the firm [2, 6, 77]. This independent variable is estimated for the year ending in 2018. A one-year lag in the measurement accounts for information assimilation and processing by the firm and the market, ensuring that stock market reactions are due to *Multiple National Cultures* prior to the pandemic.

Dependent Variables. *Quarterly Abnormal Return* of a stock is the dependent variable in our study. It measures the performance of a firm during the first quarter of 2020, at the onset of the COVID-19 pandemic. It is estimated by taking a difference between the logarithm of the stock's gross quarterly return and the CAPM beta times the logarithm of the market's gross quarterly return over the first quarter of 2020. Using the market model, the CAPM beta for each stock of a firm is estimated using returns from the year 2017 to 2019, and the returns on the S&P 500 index is used for the market index.

Table 1. Summary statistics

Variable	Mean	Std. Dev.	Distribution		
			10th	50th	90th
Multiple National Cultures	39.30	17.35	2.80	46.14	52.62
BI Systems (BIS)	0.73	0.50	0.00	1.00	1.00
Quarterly Abnormal Returns	-25.10	31.37	-66.07	-19.74	7.31
Tobin's Q	1.89	1.19	1.01	1.41	3.43
Firm Size	9.63	0.97	8.63	9.45	11.08
Cash	0.09	0.10	0.01	0.05	0.21
Leverage	0.34	0.18	0.11	0.33	0.57
Return on Equity (ROE)	0.13	0.64	-0.08	0.13	0.45
Advertising	0.01	0.02	0.00	0.00	0.02
Historical Volatility	1.79	0.77	1.04	1.58	2.69
Dividend	2.20	2.09	0.00	1.90	4.43

Control Variables. Our regression specification includes a wide set of variables that control for several firm characteristics and industry. In line with prior literature, firm level control variables are Tobin's Q, Firm Size, Cash, Leverage, Return on Equity (ROE), Advertising Expenditures, Historical Stock Volatility, Dividends and Liquidity [9, 78]. All controls are measured in 2019 US dollars.

4.4 Descriptive Statistics

Our sample and variables are at the firm level and the descriptive statistics of these measures are summarized in Table 1. The sample includes a wide distribution of firm sizes (measured in quantum of sales), with values ranging from $5.6 billion (tenth percentile) to $64.8 billion (ninetieth percentile).

About 98% of the firms in our sample have more than twenty-five subsidiaries, and 18% of firms have more than 750 subsidiaries. About 46% of the firms in our sample have a presence in more than 10 countries. The firms are widely distributed in all the industry groups, around 15% in manufacturing groups, 12% in high-tech industries, 15% in shops and services, and 6% in energy sector. The country-wise distribution of the total number of firms' subsidiaries is depicted in a heat map and shown in Fig. 1. The number of firms present in different number of countries is shown in Fig. 2.

Fig. 1. Country-wise distribution of firms' subsidiaries

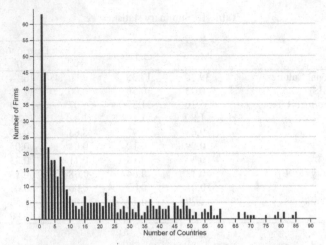

Fig. 2. Presence of firms in different number of countries

5 Results

A hierarchical regression specification is employed to test our hypothesis. Since our dependent variable, *Quarterly Abnormal Returns*, does not possess any specific properties (i.e., it is not a choice or count variable), we utilize *ordinary least squares* (OLS) specifications. We run the regression specifications (Eq. 2) with and without industry fixed effects based on the industry group of each firm. The *Breusch-Pagan* test for heteroskedasticity rejects the null hypothesis that the errors are homoscedastic in all the models. Therefore, we utilize standard errors that are robust to heteroscedasticity across all our regression specifications. Furthermore, multicollinearity is not a concern in any of the models, as assessed by *Variance Inflation Factor*, which are all less than 3. To control for outliers, all the variables used in the regression models are winsorized at the 1st and the 99th percentile. Standardized regression coefficients and robust standard errors are reported in all results tables presented hereafter, and thus regression constants are omitted.

Table 2 presents the estimation results for the direct effects of *Business Intelligence Systems* and *Multiple National Cultures* on firm performance. First, we examine the direct effect of *Business Intelligence Systems* in isolation. Column 1 and 2 presents the results of the analysis of direct effects of *Business Intelligence Systems*, using cross-sectional regressions of firms' *Quarterly Abnormal Returns*. Column 1 presents the results using *Business Intelligence Systems* along with a set of variables to control for several firm characteristics that are known to affect firm performance and in Column 2, we augment our analysis by including industry effects. In Column 1 we find the direct effect of *Business Intelligence Systems* is 0.06 ($p < 0.1$), which is positive and significant, while after including industry effects in Column 2, the coefficient of *Business Intelligence Systems* increases to 0.07 ($p < 0.1$) and is again positive and significant. This suggests support for hypothesis 1.

Table 2. Analysis of direct effects on firm performance

Variables	(1) Firm Perf.	(2) Firm Perf.	(3) Firm Perf.	(4) Firm Perf.
BI Systems	0.06*	0.07*		
	(2.85)	(2.90)		
Multiple National Cultures			0.10**	0.08*
			(0.10)	(0.09)
Observations	440	440	363	363
R-squared	0.24	0.27	0.26	0.31
Industry Dummies	No	Yes	No	Yes
F	15.08***	12.90***	13.24***	12.17***
F change	-	8.07***	-	6.08***

Notes: 1) *** p<0.01, ** p<0.05, * p<0.1; 2) Control variables included in all models.

Next, we analyze the direct effects of *Multiple National Cultures* on firms' *Quarterly Abnormal Returns*. Column 3 presents the results when *Multiple National Cultures* is used as the explanatory variable along with variables to control for firm characteristics. Additionally in Column 4, we include dummy variables that capture industry-level effects (Industry Dummies). The regression coefficients for these dummy variables are omitted for brevity. In Column 3 we find the coefficient of *Multiple National Cultures* is 0.10 (p < 0.05), which is positive and significant, while after including industry fixed effects in Column 4, the coefficient of *Multiple National Cultures* decreases to 0.08 (p < 0.1) but remains positive and significant. This supports hypothesis 2.

The estimation results for the test of our third hypothesis is presented in Table 3. A hierarchical regression model is used, beginning with inclusion of the direct effects of both *Business Intelligence Systems* and *Multiple National Cultures*, as shown in Column 1. We observe the direct effect of *Multiple National Cultures* is 0.09 (p < 0.1) and *Business Intelligence Systems* is 0.05. Both the direct effects are in the same direction but only *Multiple National Cultures* is significant. The interaction between *Multiple National Cultures* and *Business Intelligence Systems* is included in Column 2, while industry fixed effects are not. We find the coefficient for *Multiple National Cultures* * *Business Intelligence Systems* is −0.29 (p < 0.05), negative and significant. This interaction effect is also tested using the *F* test for change in R-square, the *F-change* value being 5.14, which is significant at the 5% level. After including the industry fixed effects, in Column 3 we observe the coefficient for *Multiple National Cultures* * *Business Intelligence Systems* is −0.24 (p < 0.05). Simultaneously, the direct effects of both *Business Intelligence Systems* and *Multiple National Cultures* are also positive and significant, and the *F-change* value for the test of interaction effect is 5.92, which is again significant at the 5% level.

Table 3. Analysis of interaction effects on firm performance

Variables	(1) Firm Perf.	(2) Firm Perf.	(3) Firm Perf.
BI Systems	0.05	0.27**	0.25**
	(3.46)	(7.99)	(7.90)
Multiple National Cultures	0.09*	0.22***	0.18**
	(0.10)	(0.15)	(0.15)
Multiple National Cultures * BIS		-0.29**	-0.24**
		(0.18)	(0.18)
Observations	363	363	363
R-squared	0.26	0.28	0.32
Industry Dummies	No	No	Yes
F	12.07***	11.51***	10.93***
F change	-	5.14**	5.92***

Notes: 1) *** $p<0.01$, ** $p<0.05$, * $p<0.1$; 2) Control variables included in all models.

These results in Table 3 validate our third hypothesis. The magnitude of the coefficient for the interaction effect of *Business Intelligence Systems* on *Multiple National Cultures* suggests that, at the mean value of *Multiple National Cultures*, one standard deviation increase in *Business Intelligence Systems*, negatively moderates the direct effect of *Multiple National Cultures* and is associated with lowering quarterly stock return by 7.53% (-0.24×31.37) on average. The implication of the negative result is that concurrent knowledge accruing from *Business Intelligence Systems* and *Multiple National Cultures* leads to the problem of infobesity and weakens the effect of the other on firm performance.

6 Conclusion

Our study makes two salient contributions. First, prior literature has highlighted how IT enables firms to overcome the negative consequences of multiple cultures, often with favorable results [3, 10, 54, 79]. We contribute to this conversation by demonstrating that multiple cultures also have a direct impact on performance which is reduced when business intelligence systems are simultaneously used. Second, this study joins the stream of research which examines culture and GREAT contexts in IS [1, 10, 17, 24, 42, 80, 81]. Though there have been notable advances to this stream of literature, it is still in a nascent stage. Thus, our study moves this work forward substantively.

From a practice, the findings of our study imply that managers must seek a balance between their use of *Business Intelligence Systems* and the diversity of *Multiple National Cultures* within their firm due to the potential rise of infobesity.

References

1. Ramakrishnan, T., Kathuria, A., Khuntia, J.: An empirical investigation of analytics capabilities in the supply chain. In: Lang, K.R., et al. (eds.) Smart Business: Technology and Data Enabled Innovative Business Models and Practices, vol. 403, pp. 56–63. Springer, Cham (2020). https://doi.org/10.1007/978-3-030-67781-7_6
2. Ramakrishnan, T., Khuntia, J., Kathuria, A., Saldanha, T.J.V.: An integrated model of business intelligence & analytics capabilities and organizational performance. Commun. Assoc. Inf. Syst. **46**, 31 (2020)
3. Saldanha, T.J.V., Sahaym, A., Mithas, S., Andrade-Rojas, M.G., Kathuria, A., Lee, H.-H.: Turning liabilities of global operations into assets: IT-enabled social integration capacity and exploratory innovation. Inf. Syst. Res. **31**, 361–382 (2020)
4. Karhade, P., Dong, J.Q.: Innovation outcomes of digitally enabled collaborative problemistic search capability. MIS Q. **45**, 693–717 (2021)
5. Andrade-Rojas, M.G., Kathuria, A., Konsynski, B.R.: Competitive brokerage: how information management capability and collaboration networks act as substitutes. J. Manag. Inf. Syst. **38**, 667–703 (2021)
6. Jaiswal, A., Malik, O., Karhade, P., Kathuria, A.: Too many cooks spoil the broth: infobesity in multicultural firms during Covid-19. In: Proceedings of the 55th Hawaii International Conference on System Sciences (2022)
7. Bharadwaj, A.S., Bharadwaj, S.G., Konsynski, B.R.: Information technology effects on firm performance as measured by Tobin's q. Manage. Sci. **45**, 1008–1024 (1999)
8. Hofstede, G.: Culture and organizations. Int. Stud. Manag. Organ. **10**, 15–41 (1980)
9. Andrade Rojas, M.G., Kathuria, A., Lee, H.-H.: Attaining operating performance through Pas De Trios of IT, competitive brokerage and innovation. In: International Conference on Information Systems (ICIS) (2015)
10. Karhade, P., Kathuria, A., Konsynski, B.: When Choice matters: assortment and participation for performance on digital platforms. In: Proceedings of the 54th Hawaii International Conference on System Sciences (2021)
11. Shin, D., Hasse, V.C., Schotter, A.P.J.: Multinational enterprises within cultural space and place: integrating cultural distance and tightness-looseness. Acad. Manag. J. **60**, 904–921 (2017)
12. Beugelsdijk, S., Kostova, T., Kunst, V.E., Spadafora, E., van Essen, M.: Cultural distance and firm internationalization: a meta-analytical review and theoretical implications. J. Manag. **44**, 89–130 (2018)
13. Kogut, B., Singh, H.: The effect of national culture on the choice of entry mode. J. Int. Bus. Stud. **19**, 411–432 (1988)
14. Purkayastha, S., Donnelly, R., Manolova, T.S., Edelman, L.F.: More money or more people? Institutional distance, slack resources, and EMNE internationalization. Acad. Manag. Proc. **2020**, 20205 (2020)
15. Kathuria, R., Kathuria, N.N., Kathuria, A.: Mutually supportive or trade-offs: an analysis of competitive priorities in the emerging economy of India. J. High Technol. Managem. Res. **29**, 227–236 (2018)
16. Khuntia, J., Kathuria, A., Andrade-Rojas, M.G., Saldanha, T., Celly, N.: How foreign and domestic firms differ in leveraging IT-enabled supply chain information integration in BOP markets: the role of supplier and client business collaboration. J. Assoc. Inf. Syst. **22**, 6 (2021)
17. Karhade, P., Kathuria, A.: Missing impact of ratings on platform participation in India: a call for research in GREAT domains. Commun. Assoc. Inf. Syst. **47**, 19 (2020)
18. Khuntia, J., Kathuria, A., Saldanha, T.J.V., Konsynski, B.R.: Benefits of IT-enabled flexibilities for foreign versus local firms in emerging economies. J. Manag. Inf. Syst. **36**, 855–892 (2019)

19. Dong, J.Q., Karhade, P.P., Rai, A., Xu, S.X.: How firms make information technology investment decisions: toward a behavioral agency theory. J. Manag. Inf. Syst. **38**, 29–58 (2021)
20. Tarafdar, M., Tu, Q., Ragu-Nathan, T.S.: Impact of technostress on end-user satisfaction and performance. J. Manag. Inf. Syst. **27**, 303–334 (2010)
21. Stich, J.-F., Tarafdar, M., Stacey, P., Cooper, S.C.: Appraisal of email use as a source of workplace stress: a person-environment fit approach. J. Assoc. Inf. Syst. **20**, 2 (2019)
22. Hemp, P.: Death by information overload. Harv. Bus. Rev. **87**, 82–89 (2009)
23. Eppler, M.J., Mengis, J.: The concept of information overload: a review of literature from organization science, accounting, marketing, MIS, and related disciplines. Inf. Soc. **20**, 325–344 (2004)
24. Karhade, P., Kathuria, A., Malik, O., Konsynski, B.: Digital platforms and infobesity: a research agenda. In: Garimella, A., Karhade, P., Kathuria, A., Liu, X., Xu, J., Zhao, K. (eds.) The Role of e-Business during the Time of Grand Challenges, pp. 67–74. Springer International Publishing, Cham (2021). https://doi.org/10.1007/978-3-030-79454-5_7
25. Jackson, T.W., Farzaneh, P.: Theory-based model of factors affecting information overload. Int. J. Inf. Manage. **32**, 523–532 (2012)
26. Andrade Rojas, M., Kathuria, A.: Competitive brokerage, information technology and internal resources. In: International Conference on Information Systems (2021)
27. Ramakrishnan, T., Kathuria, A., Khuntia, J.: Business analytics capability and supply chain management. In: Proceedings of the Americas Conference on Information Systems (2018)
28. Ramakrishnan, T., Khuntia, J., Kathuria, A., Saldanha, T.J.V.: Business intelligence capabilities. In: Deokar, A.V., Gupta, A., Iyer, L.S., Jones, M.C. (eds.) Analytics and Data Science, pp. 15–27. Springer, Cham (2018). https://doi.org/10.1007/978-3-319-58097-5_3
29. Wagner, H.-T., Beimborn, D., Weitzel, T.: How social capital among information technology and business units drives operational alignment and IT business value. J. Manag. Inf. Syst. **31**, 241–272 (2014)
30. Kathuria, A., Saldanha, T., Khuntia, J., Rojas, M.: How Information management capability affects innovation capability and firm performance under turbulence: evidence from India. In: International Conference on Information Systems (2016)
31. Dong, J.Q., He, J., Karhade, P.: The Penrose effect in resource investment for innovation: evidence from information technology and human capital. In: European Conference on Information Systems Proceedings (2013)
32. Dong, J.Q., Karhade, P., Rai, A., Xu, S.X.: Dynamic adjustment of information technology, corporate governance, and firm profitability. In: European Conference on Information Systems Proceedings (2013)
33. Dong, J.Q., Karhade, P., Rai, A., Xu, S.X.: Information technology in innovation activity of the firm: theory and synthesis. In: European Conference on Information Systems Proceedings (2013)
34. Mithas, S., Ramasubbu, N., Sambamurthy, V.: How information management capability influences firm performance. MIS Q. **35**, 237–256 (2011)
35. Ramakrishnan, T., Kathuria, A., Saldanha, T.J.: Business intelligence and analytics (BI&A) capabilities in healthcare. In: Theory and Practice of Business Intelligence in Healthcare, pp. 1–17. IGI Global (2020)
36. Malik, O., Karhade, P., Kathuria, A., Jaiswal, A., Yen, B.: Unravelling the origins of infobesity: the impact of frequency on intensity. In: Proceedings of the 55th Hawaii International Conference on System Sciences (2022)
37. Cho, W., Malik, O., Karhade, P., Kathuria, A.: Need for speed in the sharing economy: how IT capability drives innovation speed? In: Proceedings of the 55th Hawaii International Conference on System Sciences (2022)

38. Malik, O., Jaiswal, A., Kathuria, A., Karhade, P.: Leveraging BI systems to overcome infobesity: a comparative analysis of incumbent and new entrant firms. In: Proceedings of the 55th Hawaii International Conference on System Sciences (2022)
39. Garimella, A., Karhade, P., Kathuria, A., Liu, X., Xu, J., Zhao, K. (eds.): The Role of e-Business during the Time of Grand Challenges, vol. 418. Springer, Cham (2021). https://doi.org/10.1007/978-3-030-79454-5
40. Malik, O., Karhade, P., Kathuria, A.: How technology use drives infobesity: an in-depth look at ERP systems. In: Pacific Asia Conference on Information Systems (2021)
41. Pradhan, A., Kathuria, A., Khuntia, J.: Partner informedness, relational capability, and performance of small and large firms. In: Proceedings of the Americas Conference on Information Systems (2021)
42. Karhade, P., Kathuria, A., Dasgupta, A., Malik, O., Konsynski, B.R.: Decolonization of digital platforms: a research agenda for GREAT domains. In: Garimella, A., Karhade, P., Kathuria, A., Liu, X., Xu, J., Zhao, K. (eds.) The Role of e-Business during the Time of Grand Challenges, pp. 51–58. Springer International Publishing, Cham (2021). https://doi.org/10.1007/978-3-030-79454-5_5
43. Saldanha, T.J.V., Kathuria, A., Khuntia, J., Konsynski, B.R.: Ghosts in the machine: how marketing and human capital investments enhance customer growth when innovative services leverage self-service technologies. Inf. Syst. Res. **33**, 76–109 (2022)
44. Vijaykar, S., Karhade, P.: Remote virtual workplaces in the pandemic: the case of IT-enabled service leadership. In: Pacific Asia Conference on Information Systems (2021)
45. Vijaykar, S., Karhade, P., Gupta, M.: Work-from-home vs. work-at-home: a strategic conundrum in the digital age. In: Americas Conference on Information Systems (2021)
46. Ketokivi, M., Mahoney, J.T.: Transaction cost economics as a theory of supply chain efficiency. Prod. Oper. Manag. **29**, 1011–1031 (2020)
47. Stauffer, J.M., Kumar, S.: Impact of incorporating returns into pre-disaster deployments for rapid-onset predictable disasters. Prod. Oper. Manag. **30**, 451–474 (2021)
48. Ramakrishnan, T., Khuntia, J., Kathuria, A., Saldanha, T.J.: Business intelligence capabilities and effectiveness: an integrative model. In: Hawaii International Conference on System Sciences, pp. 5022–5031 (2016)
49. Ghemawat, P.: Managing differences: the central challenge of global strategy. Harvard Bus. Rev. **85**, 58–68, 140 (2007)
50. Arregle, J.-L., Miller, T.L., Hitt, M.A., Beamish, P.W.: How does regional institutional complexity affect MNE internationalization? J. Int. Bus. Stud. **47**, 697–722 (2016)
51. Morosini, P., Shane, S., Singh, H.: National cultural distance and cross-border acquisition performance. J. Int. Bus. Stud. **29**, 137–158 (1998)
52. Gray, J.V., Massimino, B.: The effect of language differences and national culture on operational process compliance. Prod. Oper. Manag. **23**, 1042–1056 (2014)
53. Reus, T.H., Lamont, B.T.: The double-edged sword of cultural distance in international acquisitions. J. Int. Bus. Stud. **40**, 1298–1316 (2009)
54. Saldanha, T., Kathuria, A., Khuntia, J., Konsynski, B.: It's a dangerous business, going out your door: overcoming institutional distances through IS. In: International Conference on Information Systems (2021)
55. Choi, S., Ko, I.: Leveraging electronic collaboration to promote interorganizational learning. Int. J. Inf. Manage. **32**, 550–559 (2012)
56. Sutcliffe, K.M., Weick, K.E.: Information Overload Revisited. Oxford University Press, The Oxford Handbook of Organizational Decision Making (2009)
57. Kathuria, A., Khuntia, J., Karhade, P., Ning, X.: Don't ever take sides with anyone against the family: family ownership and information management. In: Americas Conference on Information Systems (2019)

58. Ning, X., Khuntia, J., Kathuria, A., Karhade, P.: Information technology investment, environmental hostility, and firm performance: the roles of family ownership in an emerging economy. In: Hawaii International Conference on System Sciences (2020)
59. Ning, X., Khuntia, J., Kathuria, A., Karhade, P.: Ownership and management control effects on it investments: a study of Indian family firms. In: International Conference on Information Systems (2020)
60. Saldanha, T.J., Kathuria, A., Khuntia, J.: Digital service flexibility and performance of credit unions. In: Americas Conference on Information Systems (2013)
61. Brown, S.J., Warner, J.B.: Using daily stock returns: the case of event studies. J. Financ. Econ. **14**, 3–31 (1985)
62. Flammer, C.: Does corporate social responsibility lead to superior financial performance? A regression discontinuity approach. Manag. Sci. **61**, 2549–2568 (2015)
63. Ramelli, S., Wagner, A.F.: Feverish stock price reactions to COVID-19. Rev. Corp. Finan. Stud. **9**, 622–655 (2020)
64. Hendricks, K.B., Singhal, V.R.: The effect of supply chain glitches on shareholder wealth. J. Oper. Manag. **21**, 501–522 (2003)
65. Hendricks, K.B., Jacobs, B.W., Singhal, V.R.: Stock market reaction to supply chain disruptions from the 2011 great east Japan earthquake. Manuf. Serv. Oper. Manag. **22**, 683–699 (2020)
66. Mithas, S., Whitaker, J., Tafti, A.: Information technology, revenues, and profits: exploring the role of foreign and domestic operations. Inf. Syst. Res. **28**, 430–444 (2017)
67. Pincus, M., Tian, F., Wellmeyer, P., Xu, S.X.: Do Clients' enterprise systems affect audit quality and efficiency? Contemp. Account. Res. **34**, 1975–2021 (2017)
68. Dewan, S., Ren, F.: Information technology and firm boundaries: impact on firm risk and return performance. Inf. Syst. Res. **22**, 369–388 (2011)
69. Jia, N., Rai, A., Xu, S.X.: Reducing capital market anomaly: the role of information technology using an information uncertainty lens. Manage. Sci. **66**, 979–1001 (2020)
70. Forman, C.: The corporate digital divide: determinants of internet adoption. Manage. Sci. **51**, 641–654 (2005)
71. Ramakrishnan, T., Kathuria, A., Khuntia, J.: Business analytics capability and supply chain management. In: Americas Conference on Information Systems (2018)
72. Gomez-Mejia, L.R., Makri, M., Kintana, M.L.: Diversification decisions in family-controlled firms. J. Manage. Stud. **47**, 223–252 (2010)
73. Rosenzweig, P.M., Singh, J.V.: Organizational environments and the multinational enterprise. Acad. Manag. Rev. **16**, 340–361 (1991)
74. Hewett, K., Roth, M.S., Roth, K.: Conditions influencing headquarters and foreign subsidiary roles in marketing activities and their effects on performance. J. Int. Bus. Stud. **34**, 567–585 (2003)
75. Campbell, J.T., Eden, L., Miller, S.R.: Multinationals and corporate social responsibility in host countries: does distance matter? J. Int. Bus. Stud. **43**, 84–106 (2012)
76. Hofstede, G., Hofstede, G.J., Minkov, M.: Cultures and Organizations: Software of the Mind, 3rd Edition. McGraw-Hill Education (2010)
77. Gomez-Mejia, L.R., Palich, L.E.: Cultural diversity and the performance of multinational firms. J. Int. Bus. Stud. **28**, 309–335 (1997)
78. Ning, X., Khuntia, J., Kathuria, A., Konsynski, B.R.: Artificial Intelligence (AI) and cognitive apportionment for service flexibility. In: Xu, J.J., Zhu, B., Liu, X., Shaw, M.J., Zhang, H., Fan, M. (eds.) The Ecosystem of e-Business: Technologies, Stakeholders, and Connections, vol. 357, pp. 182–189. Springer, Cham (2019). https://doi.org/10.1007/978-3-030-22784-5_18
79. Kathuria, A., Saldanha, T., Khuntia, J., Andrade Rojas, M.G., Hah, H.: Strategic intent, contract duration, and performance: evidence from micro-outsourcing. In: International Conference on Information Systems (ICIS) (2015)

80. Ning, X., Karhade, P., Kathuria, A., Khuntia, J.: Influence of ownership and management on IT investment in Indian family firms. In: Lang, K.R., et al. (eds.) Smart Business: Technology and Data Enabled Innovative Business Models and Practices, vol. 403, pp. 185–193. Springer, Cham (2020). https://doi.org/10.1007/978-3-030-67781-7_17
81. Dasgupta, A., Karhade, P., Kathuria, A., Konsynski, B.: Holding space for voices that do not speak: design reform of rating systems for platforms in GREAT economies. In: Proceedings of the 54th Hawaii International Conference on System Sciences (2021)

Exploring Freelancer Attributes with Peer Endorsements

Sambit Tripathi[1]([⊠]), Amit Deokar[1], and Prasanna Karhade[2]

[1] University of Massachusetts Lowell, Lowell, MA 01854, USA
sambit_tripathi@student.uml.edu
[2] University of Hawai'i at Manoa, Honolulu, HI 96822, USA

Abstract. Online freelancing markets connect buyers with workers globally to assign various categories of tasks. A worker's quality on the platform could be assessed by their past performance (reputation systems), skills, and experience. However, these methods cannot provide insights about the worker quality in case of newly acquired skills or new workers participating on the platform. An endorsement system can be particularly instrumental in such cases by gathering and sharing endorsements of skills given to a worker by other workers. We investigate how endorsements received by a worker from their peers relate to their attributes. Drawing on social value orientation theory, we determine worker category from the past endorsement activity. Next, we apply the decision tree induction method to extract the worker attributes that are related to endorsement decisions across all worker categories. Finally, we frame our propositions based on the extracted rules.

Keywords: User-generated content · Endorsements · Social value orientation theory · Online labor markets

1 Introduction

User-generated content (UGC) is an important feature of the Internet, affecting the behavior of individuals or organizations on digital platforms. UGC helps in making purchase decisions and product sales (Chevalier and Mayzlin 2006), investment decisions (Park et al. 2014), provides hedonic value (Leung 2009), and gathers customer information for organizations (Lee and Bradlow 2011). Americans spent 58 min per day on the Facebook app and Gen-Z clocked more than 9 h of screen time per day in 2021[1]. Social media websites, e-commerce marketplaces, and other digital platforms rely on both generation and consumption of UGC to remain competitive in the industry. Yet, UGC suffers from an underprovisioning problem because UGC is a public good and is created voluntarily (Chen et al. 2010). So, platforms owners need to understand the factors that motivate users to produce UGC.

---

[1] https://www.forbes.com/sites/petersuciu/2021/06/24/americans-spent-more-than-1300-hours-on-social-media/?sh=4976a9a72547.

© Springer Nature Switzerland AG 2022
S. Fan et al. (Eds.): WeB 2021, LNBIP 443, pp. 30–42, 2022.
https://doi.org/10.1007/978-3-031-04126-6_3

Prior studies on UGC have explored three different major topics: effects of UGC, antecedents of UGC characteristics, and UGC production. Research in UGC production has primarily focused on constructs belonging to reputation systems (Burtch et al. 2018) and knowledge-related content (Gallus 2017). However, to the best of our knowledge, currently no research study focuses on the production of skill endorsements (one type of UGC) in online freelance markets.

Online freelance markets like Freelancer, Upwork, Fiverr, and PeoplePerHour are becoming prevalent in the digital gig economy connecting buyers with sellers (contract workers or freelancers), regardless of their location, to assign various genres of tasks. Buyers primarily rely on a reputation system to evaluate workers based on their historical gig performance. However, rating scores and reviews tend to be overly positive and inflated (Filippas et al. 2018; Hu et al. 2012). Yet, worker skills and expertise can be used to evaluate the worker, thus impacting their chances of getting hired in the future (Kokkodis and Ipeirotis 2014).

The skills of a worker could be evaluated by looking at historical gigs or with the help of an endorsement system. The quality of workers' skillsets can be acknowledged by the worker community with the help of an endorsement system. In an endorsement system, each user can endorse another user's skills or can receive endorsements from other users. So, endorsements are one type of UGC which are generated voluntarily to help workers improve their gig performance in an online freelance market.

The workers participating in the online freelancer markets compete against each other to acquire more freelancing/gig opportunities and maximize their income. Appreciating the competition in the form of endorsing skills presents an interesting behavior among gig workers. What attributes of worker are related to a worker's decision on endorsing his competitors?

We apply the social value orientation (SVO) theory to understand the endorsement behavior among gig workers. In social psychology, SVO deals with the "weights" that an individual may place on others' welfare versus their own welfare (Van Lange 1999). There are four categories of SVO: altruistic, cooperative, individualistic, and competitive. In the context of endorsements, an altruistic worker will only send endorsements to other workers without receiving any endorsements back since they believe in maximizing others' outcomes at cost of their own outcome. A cooperative worker will receive endorsements as well as endorse their peers because they believe in maximizing his own as well as others' outcomes. Finally, an individualistic worker will only receive endorsements and not endorse anyone as they are not concerned about peer outcomes. As competitive workers try to maximize their outcome at the cost of others' outcomes, endorsement behavior will apply to them.

The endorsed worker is assumed to have some SVO which is determined from their historical endorsement behavior. Also, a worker analyzes their peer's profile before endorsing them. The worker's profile in a digital platform lists out certain worker attributes that could be influential in the endorsement decision. These attributes will reveal the important attributes related to a specific type of worker (type of SVO). In other words, we explore the how endorsements received by a worker from their peers relate to their own attributes.

We address our research question by focusing on the endorsements generated in an online freelance marketplace. We used a global online freelance marketplace that utilizes a reputation system along with an endorsement system to help buyers meet and select the best workers for their tasks or jobs. An individual can endorse a worker by sending a personalized message along with the specific skills of the worker to be endorsed. The same worker can also endorse back the individual based on the particular individual's skills.

We collected the endorsement interactions among 90K workers in the month of May 2021 and September 2021. Approximately 9100 new endorsements were generated among these workers in three months. We also collected the endorsed worker attributes like historical endorsements, gig activity, platform activity, and location among others.

We apply the decision tree induction approach to determine what attributes attract endorsements from other workers. Tree induction is a data-driven methodology to find out patterns in the form of interpretable if-else rules. Here, we present the worker attributes (predictors) in the form of simple if-else rules that influence the decision to endorse a certain type of worker. So, the class attribute is the worker's SVO behavior and the worker attributes form the predictors. This method has been used in IS research to mine decision rules used by restaurants to participate in digital platforms (Kathuria et al. 2020) as well as IS portfolio prioritization (Karhade et al. 2015).

The results from the decision tree show 6 distinct rules which show the specific worker attributes that influence the endorsements. We derive four propositions from these six rules. The first proposition shows that the endorsements are generated with the hope that the workers receive endorsements in the future. These endorsements are targeted at cooperative workers. The second proposition belongs to individualistic workers: endorsements are generated to seek attention from the buyers and other workers who are perceived as experts and have completed a higher number of gig activities. The third proposition belongs to cooperative workers: endorsements are generated to seek attention from buyers and with the hope that the workers receive endorsements in the future. The last proposition caters to altruistic workers: endorsements are reciprocated to workers who have endorsed in the past.

The four propositions indicate the underlying patterns of endorsing a certain type of worker. Overall, we contribute to the literature on UGC production and digital platforms by focusing on the endorsements provided by workers on online freelance platforms. We also apply social value orientation to understand the endorsement behavior of workers in a labor market. The findings of our study have practical implications for digital platform owners on exploiting the endorsements to continuously engage workers while developing a cooperative worker community. A cooperative worker community would benefit workers by more gigs and then contributing to the platform revenue. In the next section, we review the related work on UGC, online freelance platforms and SVO theory.

2   Related Work

2.1   User Generated Content

Prior studies on UGC have explored three different major themes: effects of UGC, antecedents of UGC characteristics, and UGC production. Research has focused on the effects of UGC like product sales (Hu et al. 2014; Zhu and Zhang 2010), venture capital financing (Aggarwal et al. 2012), and firm competition (Kwark et al. 2014). Second, studies have also focused on the antecedents of UGC attributes like rating (Godes and Silva 2012), review helpfulness (Zhou and Guo 2017) and, review text (Tripathi et al. 2020).

Research has also examined the UGC production mechanism by several intervention methods like financial incentives (Cabral and Li 2015), peer contribution activity (Chen et al. 2010), peer awards (Burtch et al. 2021), and performance feedback (Huang et al. 2019). Prior work has focused on users' production of online reviews (Burtch et al. 2018, Cabral and Li 2015, Khern-am-nuai et al. 2018), encyclopedic content (Gallus 2017), and knowledge exchange in question and answer communities (Goes et al. 2016). We focus on the production mechanism of a specific UGC: endorsements where the endorsements are generated by workers in online freelance platforms.

2.2 Online Freelance Platforms and Endorsements

Online freelance platforms are internet-based platforms that aim to connect buyers who need certain services to professionals (gig workers) who possess the appropriate skills to accomplish these services. Many online freelance markets have emerged, like Freelancer, Upwork, Fiverr, and PeoplePerHour, and they have attracted millions of skilled professionals across the world who complete jobs as required by the buyers. Online freelance markets offer varied types of connections and interactions between buyers and workers. (a) Workers can bid on "projects" (task requirements) posted by buyers; (b) Buyers can respond to "offers" (promoted bundled work packages) posted by the workers on the platform; (c) Buyers can connect directly with workers through the platform.

UGC developed in online freelance platforms has attracted considerable research interest. The past performance of workers (reputation) affects their probability of being hired in the future (Moreno and Terwiesch 2014). Similar to e-commerce or other marketplace platforms, online freelance platforms also offer online reviews and ratings via reputation systems that enable a buyer to provide feedback to the worker on the completed tasks. The accumulated scores and the reviews gathered by the reputation system reduce the information asymmetry (Kokkodis et al. 2015), impact hiring choices and worker earnings (Gandini et al. 2016; Yoganarasimhan 2013).

However, these reputation systems fail to capture the dynamic and multi-dimensional nature of tasks in an online platform (Kokkodis 2021). The reputation scores tend to be overly positive and inflated (Filippas et al. 2018; Hu et al. 2012). Prior studies have determined the expertise of workers in a given skill and the utility of skills given a level of expertise (Kokkodis and Ipeirotis 2014). Also, the quality of the listed skills or validating the presence of skills of a worker participating in an online freelancer market could be determined by an endorsement system.

In an endorsement system, each user can endorse another user's skills or can receive endorsements from their acquaintances present in the worker community. The presence of an endorsement system in an online freelance platform allows workers to help each other by validating their skills and generate more gigs among them. Endorsements are beneficial to platform owners in terms of generating higher platform engagement for workers and indirectly contribute to the revenue of the platform by helping workers get more projects.

Prior studies on endorsement systems have focused on the endorsements received by full-time workers who participate in professional networking platforms like LinkedIn or ResearchGate. Skill endorsements of Information Technology professionals can recommend IT jobs for Informatics Engineering graduates (Kumalasari and Susanto 2019). Virtual endorsement on LinkedIn is considered as one of the ways to self-present a professional (worker) in front of potential recruiters. A study by Rapanta and Cantoni (2017) used a survey to determine the motivation behind endorsement behavior in LinkedIn and found that the majority of professionals receive and provide endorsements without calculating the epistemic weight of knowledge authority attribution. Prior studies on endorsements as a UGC have primarily focused on its effect but have not explored its production.

In summary, the literature has focused on the production of ratings, reviews, and social media posts, across multiple types of digital platforms. Our objective is to understand the endorsement generation mechanism among workers on an online freelance platform. The production of endorsements is interesting and presents a unique paradox. Here, workers compete among each other to get more gig opportunities yet help each other by endorsing others' skills. In the next section, we try to uncover this competition-cooperation behavior of workers by applying social value orientation theory.

2.3 Social Value Orientation Theory

Social value orientation (SVO) indicates the relative priority an individual emphasizes on his welfare and that of others (Van Lange 1999). SVO theory assumes that individuals maintain a diversified preference for combinations of outcomes as they relate to the benefits derived by self and others. The diversified preference results in four categories of orientation: (a) Altruistic - Maximize others' outcomes at the cost of own outcomes, (b) Cooperative - Maximize others' outcomes and own outcomes, (c) Individualistic - Maximize own outcomes and not be concerned with other's outcomes and (d) Competitive: Maximize own outcomes at the cost of other's outcomes (Fiedler et al. 2013).

A worker endorses the skills of others yields in others' welfare in terms of higher gig opportunities. A worker maximizes their peers' outcomes (in terms of more gig work) by endorsing their skills and may receive endorsements from their peers which maximizes their own outcome. In the context of endorsements, an altruistic worker will only send endorsements to other workers without receiving any endorsements back. A cooperative worker will receive endorsements and also endorse other workers. An individualistic worker will only receive endorsements and not endorse anyone. As endorsements do not harm any worker, so a competitive SVO cannot be applied in the context of endorsements.

Now, each worker in the freelance platform will belong to a certain category SVO based on the endorsement behavior. An altruistic or cooperative worker will be primarily on the sender's side of endorsement whereas an individualistic or cooperative worker will be generally on the receiver's end. Uncovering the attributes for endorsing a specific type of worker will help us understand why a worker endorses their peer in the online freelance platform.

In social psychology, reciprocity means that individuals are cooperative and nice in response to friendly actions (Fehr and Gächter 2000). In the context of endorsements, cooperative individuals may reciprocate by "endorsing back" to a worker who endorsed him sometime in the past. So, one of the factors that influence the production of endorsements could be the type of endorsement: initiation or reciprocation. Similarly, some altruistic workers may get endorsed back in the future for endorsing certain workers.

When the endorsement type is initiation, the sender looks at the profile of the potential recipient and then decides to endorse his skills. Also, the worker profile contains several worker attributes like location, hourly rate, platform gig performance, average rating, skills, prizes won at the platform among others. So, a given worker will assess the attributes of another worker before endorsing him or her for the first time. Mining these influential attributes that attract endorsements from the worker community may show how initiation type of endorsements is produced.

3 Methodology

3.1 Context

The platform used in our study is a global online freelance marketplace that helps buyers hire workers in multiple task categories such as technology and programming, language and translation, design, photo-video-audio, social media, etc. A buyer can choose a worker in three ways: direct contact from the worker profile, selecting the workers' bids for a project or responding to the offers posted by the worker. Projects are task requirements posted by buyers, whereas offers are bundled services offered by workers. This platform reports over 100 million GBP cumulative earnings for its worker community from over a million tasks. They utilize a reputation system along with an endorsement system to help buyers meet and select the best workers for their tasks or jobs.

The endorsement system permits endorsements from other workers present in that platform or individuals outside the platform who do not have a seller account in the platform. In this case, an individual can endorse a worker by sending a personalized message along with the specific skills of the worker to be endorsed. The same worker can also endorse back (or reciprocate) the individual based on the particular individual's skills.

3.2 Data

We collected the endorsement interactions among 91K workers in two phases: May 2021 and September 2021. For each endorsement received by a worker, we collected the following details: endorser name, endorser location and endorsed skills. Next, we compared the endorsement activity of each worker and filtered out the new endorsements generated between the two phases. Approximately 9100 new endorsements were generated among these workers between May and September. For all the new endorsements, we collected the following recipient worker attributes: historical endorsements, work performance, platform activity, work category, worker reputation (ratings), response time and location from May 2021.

3.3 Constructs

1. Outcome variable: The purpose of this study is to inductively build propositions for understanding a worker's endorsement activity based on his attributes in the platform. Applying the social orientation theory in our research context, we measured the worker's SVO from his endorsement activity in three levels: individualistic, cooperative and, altruistic. We are interested in understanding a worker's decision to endorse a specific worker in an online freelance platform based on the recipient's SVO. So, our outcome variable is the SVO of the endorsed worker.
2. Endorsement type: We measured the endorsement type as reciprocate or initiate. The endorsement is coded as reciprocate when a focal worker endorses the skills of another worker, where the other worker has already endorsed the skills of the focal worker. Else, the endorsement is coded as initiate.
3. Worker location attributes: We applied natural language processing to the worker's location and combined it with the World Bank dataset to determine the country type. Country type is the income level of the worker country as determined by the world bank. We assigned the values as high, medium, and low.
4. Platform gig performance: We measured the historical gig activity of workers based on the number of buyers he worked with. A worker can complete repeated projects with the same buyer, and this creates an inherent trust within them. So, we use the number of buyers instead of the number of projects completed as our attribute for measuring the gig performance of a worker. We coded them as high (number of buyers > 5), low (number of buyers < 5), and none (number of buyers = 0).
5. Platform activity: The platform captures the last time a worker used the platform for any type of task. We coded the last active time as high when the worker has used the platform in the last 6 months or less. The value is assigned low when the worker used the platform more than 6 months ago.
6. Work category: Work category is defined as the general type of gig activity that a worker performs in the platform. The platform assigns one of the following categories to each worker: Technology & Programming; Writing & Translation; Design; Digital Marketing; Video, Photo & Image; Business; Music & Audio; Marketing, Branding & Sales; and social media.
7. Rating: A worker's rating was captured on a 5-point scale at the platform website. Certain workers did not have ratings and we coded such workers as None. A worker is coded as high when the rating is equal to 5 and low when the rating is between 1 and 5.

3.4 Decision Tree Induction

The objective of decision tree induction is to discover implicit combinations of information attributes associated with similar final decisions (Quinlan 1986). The output of decision tree induction is a set of interpretable if-else rules that shows how the combination of attributes results in the decision. We first use 10-fold cross-validation to ensure that the decision rules formed yield accurate results on unseen data. This makes the induced rules robust to unseen data formed in the future. We use the C4.5 induction algorithm to grow the tree on training data (9-partitions) and then prune the tree by validating it with the test data (last partition) as suggested by Quinlan 1986. We repeat generating and pruning trees 10 times to discover the tacit structure of the data and demonstrate the robustness of the induced rules.

In this context, we create decision trees using the constructs defined above to predict the outcome variable, which is the endorsed worker's SVO using the C4.5 algorithm and validate the decision tree using 10-fold cross-validation. The prediction accuracy of the pruned tree is assessed by applying the same rules to predict decisions for workers from the unseen data or the testing set.

4   Results

The trees presented in this study are approximations of the underlying data structure of endorsement recipients. In other words, the trees approximately represent the decision process that a worker goes through before endorsing a specific type of worker. The pruned tree presents the most important worker attribute at the top followed by lesser important attributes. The prediction accuracy of the pruned tree is 62.5% which shows that the rules can be generalizable for the endorsement decision process.

Figure 1 presents the pruned decision tree that shows the most important predictors for endorsing a specific worker type. The type of endorsement is the most important attribute in the endorsement generation process followed by the number of buyers served by a worker and the country type. Table 1 presents the top 6 rules that predict the endorsement decision-making from a worker's perspective.

Table 1. Endorsement rules generated by decision tree induction

Rule #	Rule description	Decision	Instances classified
Rule I	Endorsement Type — "Initiate" Buyers = "None"	Cooperative	~2950
Rule II	Endorsement Type = "Initiate" Buyers = "High" Income Level = "Low" or "Medium"	Cooperative	~2250
Rule III	Endorsement Type = "Initiate" Buyers = "High" Income Level = "High"	Individualistic	~1800
Rule IV	Endorsement Type = "Initiate" Buyers = "Low" Income level = "Low" or "Medium"	Cooperative	~1360
Rule V	Endorsement Type = "Initiate" Buyers = "Low" Income level = "High"	Individualistic	~650
Rule VI	Endorsement Type = "Endorse Back"	Altruistic	~120

Rule I: Most of the workers have endorsed a worker whose SVO is cooperative, which means that this endorsed worker has given endorsements to his peers. This endorsement is given for the first time to a worker who has not worked with any buyers. The general form of this rule is: endorsements are initiated towards cooperative workers who have worked with no buyers. This was the main classification rule extracted from the tree as it classified the largest majority of endorsements (around 30%).

Rule II & IV: The next two rules also classify the endorsed worker as cooperative. Here, the endorsed worker hails from low- or medium-income level countries and has worked in gig activities with at least one buyer. These endorsements are targeted to cooperative workers who have completed some amount of gig activity with the buyers and are from low- or medium-income countries.

Rule III & V: These rules classify the endorsed worker as individualistic. This worker works from high-income level countries and has worked in gig activities with at least one buyer. Individualist workers do not endorse back to other workers. Such endorsements are targeted to competitive workers who have completed some amount of gig activity with the buyers and are from high-income countries (developed countries).

Rule VI: This rule classifies the endorsed worker as altruistic. In other words, if an altruistic worker has endorsed another worker in the past, the other worker has recipro-cated to this specific altruistic worker. This type of endorsement classifies the minority of endorsements (around 1.32%).

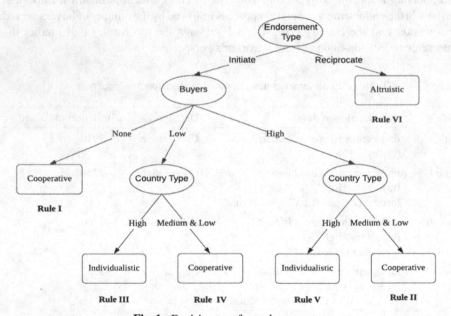

Fig. 1. Decision tree for endorsements

5 Discussion

5.1 Theoretical Propositions

In this section, we generalize the endorsements rules that were extracted from the pruned decision tree in the form of four propositions listed in Table 2. The first proposition caters to endorsements that are targeted to cooperative workers who have worked with a maximum of 5 buyers (low or none). Cooperative workers receive endorsement from their peers and endorse the skills of others. When a focal worker endorses a cooperative worker, he expects a reciprocated action from the cooperative worker in the future. This reciprocation in the form of endorsing skills to the focal worker would help him get more gig activity in the future.

The second proposition adheres to the endorsements that are targeted towards individualistic workers. An individualistic worker receives endorsements from his peers but does not endorse anyone. We found that these workers are endorsed when they belong to high-income or developed countries and have worked with at least one buyer. The workers in such countries have connections to the buyers due to the high gig activity. They are considered experts in their category of work because they belong to developed countries and have the means to train and learn specific skills. This may provide attention to the endorsing workers from buyers as well as other workers. This attention-seeking behavior might help the workers to acquire some gig activity in the future.

The third proposition focuses on the endorsements that are targeted to cooperative workers who have worked with a higher number of buyers in the online freelancing platform. Endorsing such workers may help the focal worker in seeking attention from the buyers and also have a higher expectation of receiving endorsements.

The final proposition explains the endorsement behavior when altruistic workers get endorsed. Such endorsements are reciprocated from other workers given that the focal worker has endorsed them in the past. This proposition introduces the concept of dynamic social value orientation of gig workers.

Table 2. Propositions from extracted rules

Proposition	Rule #
P1: Endorsements are generated with the hope that the workers receive endorsements in the future	Rule I & Rule IV
P2: Endorsements are generated to seek attention from the buyers and other workers who are perceived as experts and have completed a higher number of gig activities	Rule III & Rule V
P3: Endorsements are also generated to seek attention from buyers and with the hope that the workers receive endorsements in the future	Rule II
P4: Endorsements are reciprocated to workers who have endorsed in the past	Rule VI

5.2   Contributions

There are three major contributions of this study. First, we exploit social value orientation theory to understand the endorsement behavior of workers in a digital labor market. We categorize workers as individualistic, cooperative, and altruistic based on their receiving and sending endorsement statistics. Second, we use the decision tree induction method to determine the worker attributes that correlate to a worker's decision to endorse a certain type of worker. We framed four propositions from the extracted rules of the decision tree.

Third, we contribute to the literature on UGC production and digital platforms by focusing on the endorsements provided by workers on online freelance platforms. The four propositions framed in the previous section explain how worker attributes influence the generation of endorsements for a specific type of worker. Prior studies have analyzed the effect of endorsements and not on the production mechanism (Rapanta and Cantoni 2017).

The findings of our study have multiple practical implications. First, digital platform owners can use the endorsement system as a way to continuously engage workers thereby developing a cooperative worker community. A cooperative worker community would benefit workers by more gigs and then contributing to the platform revenue. Next, a cooperative worker community would help the workers continuously update their skills to compete in the freelancing market.

5.3   Limitations and Future Work

Our work has several limitations. First, the decision tree induction method does not yield the true causality of the endorsement generation mechanism. A randomized controlled experiment may reveal the causal relationship between worker attributes and their endorsement behavior. Second, the number of endorsements generated among 91K workers in 3 months was very low – 9100 endorsements. There might be a dynamic process in workers' SVO where the orientation may change over time. A future research question could be determining the attributes that influence the change of a worker's SVO over time.

6   Conclusion

In this study, we frame four propositions that describe how worker attributes are related to the generation of endorsements among them in an online freelance platform. First, we categorize workers based on the SVO theory into individualistic, cooperative, and altruistic. Next, we present how worker attributes are associated with the decision of endorsing a certain category of worker. We used the decision tree induction method on a global freelance online marketplace to discover the patterns for endorsing a certain category of worker. Our work contributes to the literature of UGC production by focusing on endorsement which was not studied in the literature.

References

Aggarwal, R., Gopal, R., Gupta, A., Singh, H.: Putting money where the mouths are: the relation between venture financing and electronic Word-of-Mouth. Inf. Syst. Res. **23**(3), 976–992 (2012)

Burtch, G., He, Q., Hong, Y., Lee, D.: How do peer awards motivate creative content? Experimental evidence from reddit. Manage. Sci., 1–19 (2021). Articles i

Burtch, G., Hong, Y., Bapna, R., Griskevicius, V.: Stimulating online reviews by combining financial incentives and social norms. Manage. Sci. **64**(5), 2065–2082 (2018)

Cabral, L., Li, L.I.: A dollar for your thoughts: feedback-conditional rebates on eBay. Manage. Sci. **61**(9), 2052–2063 (2015)

Chen, Y., Harper, F.M., Konstan, J., Li, S.X.: Social comparisons and contributions to online communities: a field experiment on MovieLens. Am. Econ. Rev. **100**(4), 1358–1398 (2010)

Chevalier, J.A., Mayzlin, D.: The effect of word of mouth on sales: online book reviews. J. Mark. Res. **43**(3), 345–354 (2006)

Fehr, E., Gächter, S.: Fairness and retaliation: the economics of reciprocity. J. Econ. Perspect. **14**(3), 159–181 (2000)

Fiedler, S., Glöckner, A., Nicklisch, A., Dickert, S.: Social value orientation and information search in social dilemmas: an eye-tracking analysis. Organ. Behav. Hum. Decis. Process. **120**(2), 272–284 (2013)

Filippas, A., Horton, J.J., Golden, J.: Reputation inflation. In: ACM EC 2018 - Proceedings 2018 ACM Conference Economics Economic Computation, pp. 483–484. Association for Computing Machinery, Inc., New York (2018)

Gallus, J.: Fostering public good contributions with symbolic awards: a large-scale natural field experiment at Wikipedia. Manage. Sci. **63**(12), 3999–4015 (2017)

Gandini, A., Pais, I., Beraldo, D.: Reputation and trust on online labour markets: the reputation economy of Elance. Work Organ. Labour Glob. **10**(1), 27–43 (2016)

Godes, D., Silva, J.C.: Sequential and temporal dynamics of online opinion. Mark. Sci. **31**(3), 448–473 (2012)

Goes, P.B., Guo, C., Lin, M.: Do incentive hierarchies induce user effort? Evid. Online Knowl. Exch. **27**(3), 497–516 (2016). https://doi.org/10.1287/isre.2016.0635

Hu, N., Bose, I., Koh, N.S., Liu, L.: Manipulation of online reviews: an analysis of ratings, readability, and sentiments. Decis. Support Syst. **52**, 674–684 (2012)

Hu, N., Koh, N.S., Reddy, S.K.: Ratings lead you to the product, reviews help you clinch it? The mediating role of online review sentiments on product sales. Decis. Support Syst. **57**(1), 42–53 (2014)

Huang, N., et al.: Motivating user-generated content with performance feedback: evidence from randomized field experiments. Manage. Sci. **65**(1), 327–345 (2019)

Karhade, P., Shaw, M.J., Subramanyam, R.: Patterns in information systems portfolio prioritization: evidence from decision tree induction. MIS Q. Manag. Inf. Syst. **39**(2), 413–433 (2015)

Kathuria, A., Karhade, P.P., Konsynski, B.R.: In the realm of hungry ghosts: multi-level theory for supplier participation on digital platforms. J. Manag. Inf. Syst. **37**(2), 396–430 (2020)

Khern-am-nuai, W., Kannan, K., Ghasemkhani, H.: Extrinsic versus intrinsic rewards for contributing reviews in an online platform **29**(4), 871–892 (2018). https://doi.org/10.1287/isre.2017.0750

Kokkodis, M.: Dynamic, multidimensional, and skillset-specific reputation systems for online work. Inf. Syst. Res. **32**(3), 688–712 (2021)

Kokkodis, M., Ipeirotis, P.G.: The utility of skills in online labor markets. In: Proceedings International Conference Information Systems 2014 (Auckland), pp. 1–18 (2014)

Kokkodis, M., Papadimitriou, P., Ipeirotis, P.G.: Hiring behavior models for online labor markets. In: WSDM 2015 - Proceedings 8th ACM International Conference Web Search Data Mining, pp. 223–232 (2015)

Kumalasari, L.D., Susanto, A.: Recommendation system of information technology jobs using collaborative filtering method based on LinkedIn skills endorsement. SISFORMA J. Inf. Syst. **6**(1), 63 (2019)

Kwark, Y., Chen, J., Raghunathan, S.: Online product reviews: implications for retailers and competing manufacturers. Inf. Syst. Res. **25**(1), 93–110 (2014)

Van Lange, P.A.M.: The pursuit of joint outcomes and equality in outcomes: an integrative model of social value orientation. J. Pers. Soc. Psychol. **77**(2), 337–349 (1999)

Lee, T.Y., Bradlow, E.T.: Automated marketing research using online customer reviews. J. Mark. Res. **48**(5), 881–894 (2011)

Leung, L.: User-generated content on the internet: an examination of gratifications, civic engagement and psychological empowerment. New Media Soc. **11**(8), 1327–1347 (2009)

Moreno, A., Terwiesch, C.: Doing business with strangers: reputation in online service marketplaces. Inf. Syst. Res. **25**(4), 865–886 (2014)

Park, J.H., Gu, B., Leung, A.C.M., Konana, P.: An investigation of information sharing and seeking behaviors in online investment communities. Comput. Hum. Behav. **31**(1), 1–12 (2014)

Quinlan, J.R.: Induction of decision trees. Mach. Learn. **1**, 81–106 (1986)

Rapanta, C., Cantoni, L.: The LinkedIn endorsement game: why and how professionals attribute skills to others. Bus. Prof. Commun. Q. **80**(4), 443–459 (2017)

Tripathi, S., Deokar, A.V., Ajjan, H.: Understanding the order effect of online review sentiments and product features. In: Proceedings 2020 Pre-ICIS SIGDSA Symposium (2020)

Yoganarasimhan, H.: The value of reputation in an online freelance marketplace. Mark. Sci. **32**(6), 860–891 (2013)

Zhou, S., Guo, B.: The order effect on online review helpfulness: a social influence perspective. Decis. Support Syst. **93**, 77–87 (2017)

Zhu, F., Zhang, X.: Impact of online consumer reviews on sales: the moderating role of product and consumer characteristics. J. Mark. **74**(2), 133–148 (2010)

Effects of COVID-19 on Critics' Rating Behavior

Thomás Peña[1], Tianxi Dong[1](✉) (iD), and Tianjie Deng[2]

[1] Michael Neidorff School of Business, Trinity University, San Antonio, USA
{tpena,tdong}@trinity.edu
[2] Department of Business Information and Analytics, Daniels College of Business,
University of Denver, Denver, USA
tianjie.deng@du.edu

Abstract. Since the beginning of the coronavirus (COVID-19) pandemic, we begin to accept this unusual time of living as the "new normal". Under unprecedented circumstances and stressors, the effects of COVID-19 may have not only shifted our ways of living but may also have had a noticeable impact on human behavior and emotions online. This study aims to investigate changes in critics' rating behavior due to the COVID-19 pandemic. Using Rotten Tomatoes, which is one of the most trusted movie critic websites, we analyzed 44,459 critic reviews to discover the changes in movie critic opinions from before to after the beginning of the COVID-19 outbreak. To capture the changes in reviews of movie critics, we analyzed the effects of COVID-19 on critic movie ratings and sentiments. This research finds that while COVID-19 is perceived to have negatively affected all our lives, critic movie ratings during the COVID-19 pandemic are slightly more positive than before the pandemic. Moreover, in analyzing movie critic reviews, there is no significant impact of COVID-19 on the change in the sentiment of movie critics. This research enlightens online movie platforms of the rating behavioral changes of movie critics before and during the pandemic.

Keywords: Critic reviews · COVID-19 · Rating behavior

1 Introduction

In the beginning of 2020, humankind faced a contagious disease outbreak like no other, the coronavirus (COVID-19) pandemic. Since its outbreak in January 2020, over 4.14 million people have died from contracting COVID-19 [4]. In trying to battle the spread of COVID-19, governments across the world guided their citizens to enter long periods of social distancing to limit human interactions. These periods of social distancing were characterized by limited physical interactions from individuals outside of a person's immediate family/friend group [10]. It's been noted that the prolonged times of self-distancing have resulted in rises in various mental health disorders, such as anxiety and depression [11].

As a result of the research detailing the impact the COVID-19 pandemic has had on mental health, this has prompted the question of how this pandemic has moreover affected online behavior. In a 2015 research article published by Pentheny [13], it found

S. Fan et al. (Eds.): WeB 2021, LNBIP 443, pp. 43–54, 2022.
https://doi.org/10.1007/978-3-031-04126-6_4

that people who were characterized as "less self-monitored" tend to trust critics' ratings and reviews for a respective movie. Therefore, knowing that movie critics can have a direct effect on consumer decisions when choosing a movie, it is important to examine the changes of behavior and sentiment of movie critics as an effect of the COVID-19 pandemic. This research serves to better understand the implications of the pandemic on possible changes in critics' ratings and sentiments.

To capture the differences in critics' rating behavior before and after the COVID-19 outbreak, we investigated critic rating and review data from Rotten Tomatoes. Through analyzing 44,459 reviews from January 1, 2019, to December 31st, 2020, across 714 movies, we were able to detect differences in rating behavior before and after the COVID-19 outbreak. We found that ratings during the COVID-19 pandemic tended to be more positive than before, however, there were no detected changes in sentiment, positive or negative, amongst critics. This research enlightens online movie platforms of the rating behavioral changes of movie critics before and during the pandemic. Moreover, this research contributes to early research looking at effects of the COVID-19 pandemic on human behavior. If examining economic implications or social perception changes within the movie industry during the pandemic, this research can serve as insight. Additionally if another unexpected event, such as the COVID-19 pandemic, were to arise in the future is research serves to explain changes in online behavior of movie critics.

In Sect. 2, we discuss the impacts of COVID-19 on human behavior and the influence of critics. In Sect. 3, we describe the data and the empirical model to analyze the effects of COVID-19 on critic rationing behavior. The results are presented in Sect. 4. The paper concludes with a discussion of our findings, implications of our findings, and suggestions for future research.

2   Literature Review

In this section, we discuss how this research is related to previous papers that researched the influence of movie critics, how COVID-19 has affected mental health globally, and how this research extends those works. Within this section, we will explain the relevance of researching and analyzing critics' rating behavior as an effect of the COVID-19 pandemic.

2.1   The Impact of COVID-19 on People's Emotions and Behaviors

Yarrington et al. [18] noted that the COVID-19 pandemic presents an unprecedented crisis on public mental health, including an increase in anxiety, stress, tiredness, and depression. The increased presence of mental disorders within the public is driven by heightened distress due to fear of contracting the COVID-19 virus, family or friends contracting the virus, economic hardships and job loss, and/or abrupt disruptions within daily life during the pandemic [16]. As diverse and varied as humans are, this is the same for how individuals dealt with the added pressure and stressors of the COVID-19 pandemic. In Yarrington's research, in surveying over 157,000 Americans on the impact of COVID-19 on personal mental health, it was found that anxiety increased during the beginning of the pandemic, and sadness and depression increased during the later months of the pandemic. On the other hand, while there were rising levels of concern for public mental health, Waters' research looks at the impact of positive psychology on humans during the COVID-19 pandemic. In their findings, subsets of individuals were able to overcome the negative emotions associated with the pandemic by implementing nine applications of positive psychology within their lives: meaning, coping, self-compassion, courage, gratitude, character strengths, positive emotions, positive interpersonal processes, and high-quality connections [16]. It is important to not only note the various psychological ways in which COVID-19 may have affected individuals, but moreover how individuals cope with added stressors and how this may transverse to online behavior. With the resumed release of new movies after COVID-19 halted movie productions, movie critics were able to find meaning, gratitude, and positive emotions online once again, traversing to higher rating behaviors. Waters describes meaning as the coherence, significance, and purpose of an individual's perceived value of themselves, in this case a movie critic's ability to contribute to the movie community, gratitude as the express appreciation of benefactors, and positive emotions as a pleasant affective state based on one's current circumstances with their internal state and external environment. After the movie-watching experience was restored with releases of new movies, movie critics found meaning, gratitude, and positive emotions to an environment resembling that of before the negative restrictions of COVID-19, leading to higher movie ratings.

2.2 Influence of Critics' Ratings on Reviews and Consumer Behavior

Critic reviews are provided by experts and offer the "wisdom of the experts", who have more specialized knowledge [15]. Extensive research has studied the impact of critics' ratings on sales and consumer reviewing behavior. According to Reddy et al. [14], critics are opinion leaders in the choice processes for consumers, and they help determine the success or failure of Broadway shows. Moreover, it is noted that in fact, critics' ratings influence the demand and popularity of movies among consumers [2, 9]. In a similar finding by Eagan, critics do have a moderate influence during big box office movie releases, and negative reviews have more influence on consumers than positive reviews [8]. In a more recent study, Basuroy et al. [3] found that critics ratings have a more influential role than user ratings on moviegoing decisions. In the research findings of Deng et al. [6], critic reviews have an overall positive effect on subsequent user reviews in terms of content quantity and quality. In specific instances when a person may be "less self-monitored," this tends to magnify the influence of critics' ratings and reviews on consumers [13]. In knowing the magnitude of influence critics can have on consumer behavior, this begs the question of the impact of critic biases on consumers. Caliendo et al. [5] found that book critics are disposed to selection biases against certain characteristics of books, such as book price, number of pages, and the gender of the author. Dobrescu et al. [7] show that professional book critics seem to favor authors who have won book prizes and have garnered other attention in the press but less favorable to first time authors. Such biases of critics translate into ratings that may hold influence over consumers. Although prior students have intensively examined the effect of critic reviews on sales and consumer behavior, the impact of the covid Within Rotten Tomatoes, critics hold a position of influence amongst consumers. As critics are noted to have a certain level of positional influence on consumer behavior, this research study tries to observe changes in critics' rating behavior as an effector of COVID-19, which would in turn influence consumer decision making.

3 Data and Methodology

3.1 Rotten Tomatoes

Rotten Tomatoes is one of the largest online review platforms for movies and television shows. With an average of 70 million unqiue user visits per month, the online platform allows both movie critics and everyday movie-goers to publish public reviews and ratings for any movie or television show. Rotten Tomatoes is most known for its tomatometer and audience score ratings. Tomatometer is the collective rating movie critics have given to a movie or television show, while audience score rating is the collective audience rating for a movie or television show. As seen in Fig. 1, *Stand and Deliver* received a tomatometer of 83% and an audience score of 79% on Rotten Tomatoes. As seen in Fig. 2, verified critics publish their reviews for individual movies. Complete critic reviews include both a written review and numeric rating based on individual movie critic evaluation.

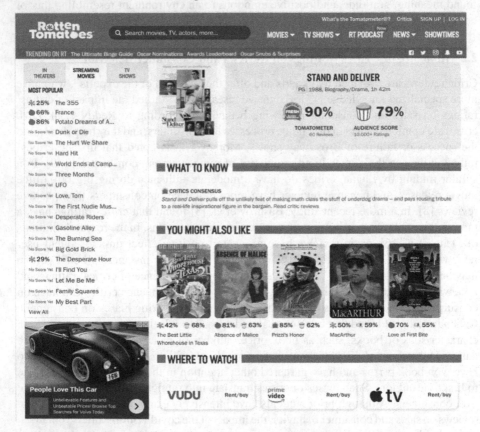

Fig. 1. Rotten Tomatoes review/ratings page

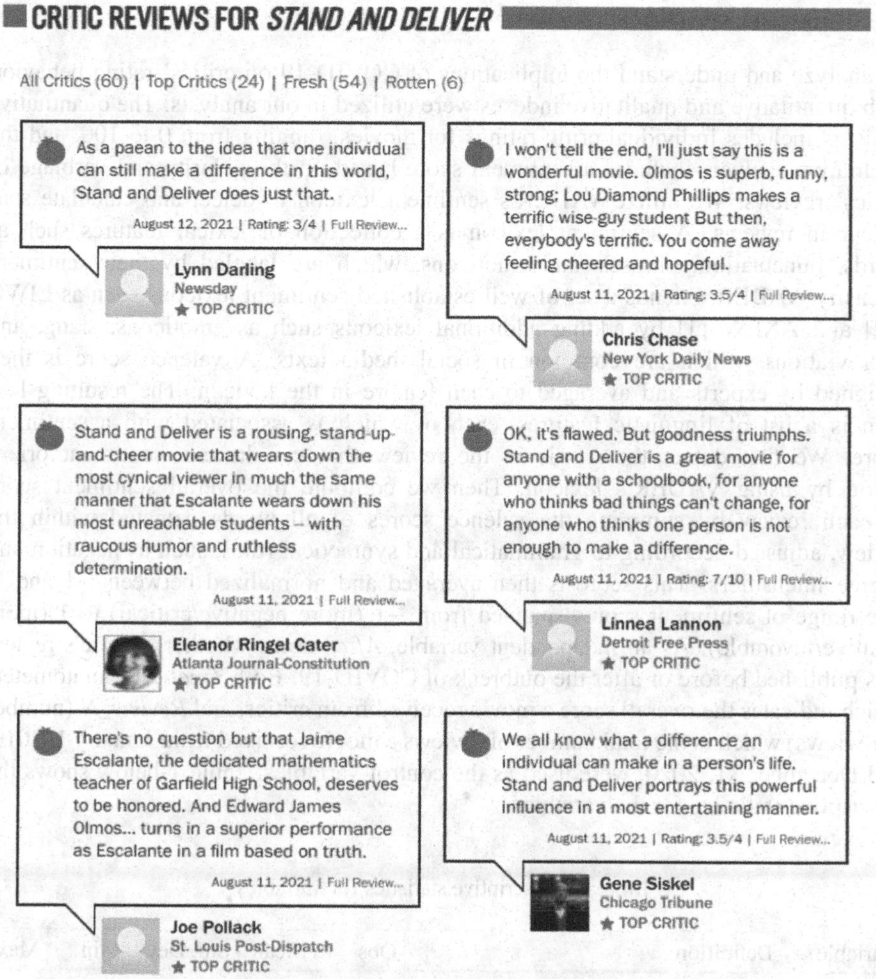

■ CRITIC REVIEWS FOR *STAND AND DELIVER* ■

All Critics (60) | Top Critics (24) | Fresh (54) | Rotten (6)

As a paean to the idea that one individual can still make a difference in this world, Stand and Deliver does just that.

August 12, 2021 | Rating: 3/4 | Full Review...

Lynn Darling
Newsday
★ TOP CRITIC

I won't tell the end, I'll just say this is a wonderful movie. Olmos is superb, funny, strong; Lou Diamond Phillips makes a terrific wise-guy student But then, everybody's terrific. You come away feeling cheered and hopeful.

August 11, 2021 | Rating: 3.5/4 | Full Review...

Chris Chase
New York Daily News
★ TOP CRITIC

Stand and Deliver is a rousing, stand-up-and-cheer movie that wears down the most cynical viewer in much the same manner that Escalante wears down his most unreachable students -- with raucous humor and ruthless determination.

August 11, 2021 | Full Review...

Eleanor Ringel Cater
Atlanta Journal-Constitution
★ TOP CRITIC

OK, it's flawed. But goodness triumphs. Stand and Deliver is a great movie for anyone with a schoolbook, for anyone who thinks bad things can't change, for anyone who thinks one person is not enough to make a difference.

August 11, 2021 | Rating: 7/10 | Full Review...

Linnea Lannon
Detroit Free Press
★ TOP CRITIC

There's no question but that Jaime Escalante, the dedicated mathematics teacher of Garfield High School, deserves to be honored. And Edward James Olmos... turns in a superior performance as Escalante in a film based on truth.

August 11, 2021 | Full Review...

Joe Pollack
St. Louis Post-Dispatch
★ TOP CRITIC

We all know what a difference an individual can make in a person's life. Stand and Deliver portrays this powerful influence in a most entertaining manner.

August 11, 2021 | Rating: 3.5/4 | Full Review...

Gene Siskel
Chicago Tribune
★ TOP CRITIC

Fig. 2. Rotten Tomatoes critics' review and rating section

In trying to analyze the change of critics' rating behavior as an effect of the COVID-19 pandemic, we reviewed data from January 1, 2019, to December 31st, 2020. As noted by the World Health Organization, the COVID-19 pandemic began on January 30, 2020, which served as the bound for data before and during the pandemic [17]. Additionally, to correctly observe the changes in critics' rating behavior, we only included ratings for movies published both before and after the COVID-19 outbreak. The final review data analyzed included 44,459 critic reviews across 714 movies to examine the change in ratings and sentiments of critics as an effect of COVID-19.

3.2 Empirical Method

To analyze and understand the implications of COVID-19 on critics' rating behavior, both quantitative and qualitative indexes were utilized in our analysis. The quantitative analysis includes individual critic ratings for movies, ranging from 0 to 100, and the qualitative analysis includes a sentiment score based on the polarity and verbiage of critics' reviews. We utilize VADER's sentiment lexicon to detect and calculate sentiment in reviews. A sentiment lexicon is a collection of lexical features such as words, punctuation, phrases, and emoticons, which are labeled by their sentiment intensity. VADER extends a set of well-established sentiment lexicons such as LIWC [12] and ANEW [1] by adding additional lexicons such as emoticons, slang, and abbreviations, which are common in social media texts. A valence score is then assigned by experts and averaged to each feature in the lexicon. The resulting lexicon is a list of linguistic features, each of which is associated with a sentiment score. We first detect the words in the review that can have a sentiment orientation by using VADER's lexicon. Then we compute the overall sentiment score of each review by summing the valence scores of all words detected within the review, adjusted according to grammatical and syntactical rules, such as negation and degree intensifiers. This score is then averaged and normalized between −1 and 1. The range of sentiment scores spanned from −1 (more negative/critical) to 1 (more positive/favorable). As an independent variable, *After* notes whether a critic's review was published before or after the outbreak of COVID-19. Both *Tmeter* (Tomatometer) which indicates the overall score a movie received from critics, and *Review_N* (number of reviews) which is the total number of reviews a movie received from January 1, 2019, and December 31, 2020, were used as the control variables. Table 1 below shows the descriptive statistics for the variables.

Table 1. Descriptive statistics for variables.

Variable	Definition	Obs	Mean	Std. Dev.	Min	Max
Dependent Variables						
Rating	Quantitative satisfaction scores an individual critic rates a movie	44,459	0.65	0.19	0	1
Sentiment	Negative/positive polarity score assigned from critics' review	44,459	0.22	0.50	−0.99	0.99
Independent Variables						
After	The value is 1 if the review is written after the start of COVID-19 (Jan 30, 2021), otherwise 0	44,459	0.40	0.49	0	1
Control Variables						
Tmeter	Overall critic score rated for individual movies	44,459	0.68	0.36	0	1
Review_N	The number of reviews for each individual movie	44,459	52.81	45.70	1	185

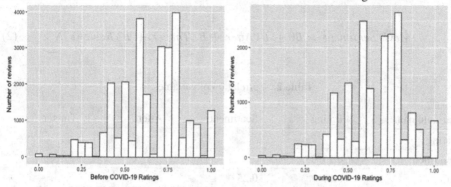

Fig. 3. Distributions of critics' ratings before and during COVID-19

Figure 3 and Fig. 4 shows the distributions of critics' ratings and sentiments before and during COVID-19. According to the figures, the frequency of scores around 0.75 during COVID-19 is slightly higher than that before COVID-19. Similarly, the frequency of sentiment scores 0.5 or above during COVID-19 is also higher than that before COVID-19. The descriptive analysis of the rating and sentiment distributions before and during COVID-19 are consistent with the two sample t-test and the regression analysis in Sect. 4.

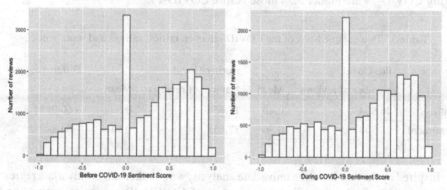

Fig. 4. Distributions of critics' sentiments before and during COVID-19

Equation 1 and Eq. 2 show the empirical model of this research. In Eq. 1, this research tries to capture behavioral changes of critics' ratings as a result of COVID-19 by comparing ratings before and after the COVID-19 outbreak by controlling *Tmeter*, and *Reviews_N*. In Eq. 2, this research tries to capture changes in critics' sentiment as a result of COVID-19 by comparing sentiment scores before and after the COVID-19 outbreak by controlling *Tmeter*, and *Reviews_N*. We control for the effects of users' ratings and review volume on critics' ratings and sentiments. Table 2 presents the correlations between variables investigated in this research.

$$Movie\ Rating = B0 + B1\ After + B2\ Tmeter + B3\ Reviews\_N \qquad (1)$$

$$Movie\ Sentiment = B0 + B1\ After + B2\ Tmeter + B3\ Reviews\_N \qquad (2)$$

Table 2. Correlation of variables.

Variable name	Rating	Sentiment	After	Tmeter
Rating				
Sentiment	0.25***			
After	0.01**	0.25***		
Tmeter	0.69***	0.26***	0.25***	
Review_N	0.13***	0.01	0.11	0.03

4 Results

Table 3 presents the t-statistics results of the comparison between critics' ratings and sentiments before and during COVID-19. The differences in critics' ratings and sentiments are both statistically significant. We can see the means of critics rating and sentiments during COVID-19 are higher than those before COVID-19.

Table 3. Two-sample t-test of the COVID effect on critics' ratings and sentiments.

Variables	Pre-Covid		During-Covid		Difference test
	Number of reviews	Mean	Number of reviews	Mean	
Ratings	26,804	0.40	17,655	0.60	−60.9***
Sentiment	26,804	0.36	17,655	0.54	−54.849***

Inspired by the results of the univariate analysis, we conducted a multivariate regression analysis to further investigate the impact of COVID-19 on critics' ratings and sentiments. Table 4 presents the results of the regression analysis which captures critics' ratings changes as an effect of the COVID-19 pandemic. The model shows that critics' ratings for movies published after the beginning of the pandemic tended to be more positive than before (0.00523, $p < 0.01$). To take a step further to understand perceptual differences after the pandemic, Table 5 presents the results of the regression which captures critics' sentiment changes as an effect of the COVID-19 pandemic. Compared to previous results, there is no analyzed correlation between change in sentiment within critics' reviews as an effect of the COVID-19 pandemic (0.003, $p = 0.529$). To sum up, before the COVID-19 pandemic, critic review ratings tended to be lower, and reviews published after the beginning of the pandemic tend to be slightly more positive. However, after evaluation of critic review sentiment scores, no significant impact of COVID-19 was detected.

Table 4. Regression analysis of the covid effect on critics' ratings.

Variables	Estimate	Std. error	T-value	P-value
After	0.00523	0.00174	3.02	<0.01***
Tmeter	0.211	0.00228	92.64	<0.01***
Review_N	0.00009541	0.0000188	5.00	<0.01***
Constant	0.504	0.00208	242.69	<0.01***

Note: Observations = 44,459.

Table 5. Regression analysis of the covid effect on critics' sentiments.

Variables	Estimate	Std. error	T-value	P-value
After	0.003	0.00501	0.63	0.529
Tmeter	0.137	0.00658	20.90	<0.01***
Review_N	0.000187	0.0000543	3.44	<0.01***
Constant	0.5	0.00208	242.69	<0.01***

Note: Observations = 44,459.

5 Discussion and Conclusion

By comparing rating and sentiment changes of critics before and after the outbreak
and COVID-19, this research contributes to understanding the impact of perceptual
differences as an effect of the pandemic. Considering the two results, critics' ratings
have changed as an effect of the COVID-19 pandemic, however, the sentiment has not.
After the beginning of the coronavirus outbreak, it can be observed that critics' behavior
did change, positively. Therefore, critics tended to be more critical with ratings before
the pandemic, and after the start of the COVID-19 pandemic, awarded higher ratings to
movies.

In looking at the results of this research analysis, the changes in critics' rating behavior can be explained by changes in future outlooks caused by the pandemic. As mentioned
by Waters et al. [16], the use of positive psychology during the pandemic changed the
mental health issues of many during the pandemic. Noting an increase of gratitude and
post-traumatic growth because of the feeling of a positive outlook coming out of the
COVID-19 pandemic, this caused changes in behavior. The changes in critic rating
behavior follow this. During the pandemic when many movie productions were shut
down, when a movie was released during the pandemic it was a symbol of a positive

outlook for the future and returning to normalcy. Waters mentions that the deployment of positive emotions during a time of uncertainty and widespread negativity, such as the COVID-19 pandemic, can serve the purpose of caring for oneself. In the case of critics' rating behavior being more positive after the COVID-19 outbreak, this could be attributed to movies being a form of a temporary distraction from reality for critics, and in return resulting in high ratings.

This research serves to inform movie platforms of the changing behaviors of critics during the COVID-19 pandemic. While increased positivity within critic ratings may be short-term, as mentioned previously about the influence of critics, movie platforms can expect to see the same shifts of behavior from consumers. When the COVID-19 era passes in the near future, there may be an expectation for critics to shift to a more critical and negative rating behavior, and resultantly consumers will follow thereafter. This research provides context to the impact of COVID-19 on critics' behavior and the indirect effect on consumer behavior. These findings raise questions about the reliability and subjectivity of critic ratings as unbiased indicators of quality. Since critic reviews are under the control of a review platform, platform stakeholders can adjust their strategies to account for possible review biases resulting from the emotional stressors.

This research, however, has several limitations. First, while this research included a sentiment score associated with a snapshot of a critic's individual review, we did not collect the full-text reviews. It may be worth investigating the full textual information to better understand how COVID-19 impacts critics' sentiments. Secondly, this research did not consider the type of films that were rated. Biases of types of movies preferred by critics may be worth investigating in conjunction with the effects of COVID-19 on critics' rating behavior. The distribution of movie genres can be found in the Appendix. Third, the time variable (*After*) is binary with a pre-defined time threshold. Maybe is better to convert the time variable to a time-delta.

Overall, this research uncovered the effects of COVID-19 on critic's rating and sentiment behavior changes. Through analyzing critic ratings from Rotten Tomatoes, it was observed that while critic sentiments did not change as an outcome of the COVID-19 pandemic, the rating behavior of critics did. Attributed to the positive outlooks of the COVID-19 pandemic, critics tended to rate movies during the COVID-19 pandemic more positively than before.

Appendix

Table A.1. Distribution of movie genres.

Movie genre	Number of observations
Action	46
Adventure	16
Animation	17
Comedy	79
Crime	16
Documentary	97
Drama	203
Family	5
Fantasy	7
History	10
Horror	56
International	84
Music	5
Mystery	4
Romance	14
Science fiction	17
Thirller	33
TV movie	1
War	3
Western	1

References

1. Bradley, M.M., Lang, P.J.: Affective norms for English words (ANEW): instruction manual and affective ratings, vol. 30, no. 1, pp. 25–36. Technical report C-1, The Center for Research in Psychophysiology, University of Florida (1999)
2. Basuroy, S., Chatterjee, S., Ravid, S.: How critical are critical reviews? The box office effects of film critics, star power, and budgets. J. Market. **67**(4) (2003). http://www.jstor.org/stable/30040552
3. Basuroy, S., Abraham Ravid, S., Gretz, R.T., Allen, B.J.: Is everybody an expert? An investigation into the impact of professional versus user reviews on movie revenues. J. Cult. Econ. **44**(1), 57–96 (2019). https://doi.org/10.1007/s10824-019-09350-7

4. CDC COVID Data Tracker Weekly Review (2021). https://www.cdc.gov/coronavirus/2019-ncov/covid-data/covidview/index.html. Accessed 19 July 2021
5. Caliendo, M., Clement, M., Shehu, E.: The effect of individual professional critics on books' sales: capturing selection biases from observable and unobservable factors. Market. Lett. **26**(4) (2015)
6. Deng, Y., Zheng, J., Khern-am-nuai, W., Kannan, K.N.: More than the quantity: the value of editorial reviews for a UGC platform. Manag. Sci. (2021, forthcoming)
7. Dobrescu, L.I., Luca, M., Motta, A.: What makes a critic tick? Connected authors and the determinants of book reviews. J. Econ. Behav. Organ. **96**, 85–103 (2013)
8. Eagan, O.: The influence of film critics. In: Oscar Buzz and the Influence of Word of Mouth on Movie Success, pp. 41–51. Springer, Cham (2020). https://doi.org/10.1007/978-3-030-41180-0_5
9. Eliashberg, J., Shugan, S.M.: Film critics: influencers or predictors? J. Mark. **61**(2), 68–78 (1997)
10. Hopkins Coronavirus, Social and Physical Distancing and Self-Quarantine (2021). https://www.hopkinsmedicine.org/health/conditions-and-diseases/coronavirus/coronavirus-social-distancing-and-self-quarantine. Accessed 19 July 2021
11. KFF: The Implications of COVID-19 for Mental Health and Substance Use (2021). https://www.kff.org/coronavirus-covid-19/issue-brief/the-implications-of-covid-19-for-mental-health-and-substance-use/. Accessed 19 July 2021
12. Pennebaker, J.W., Francis, M.E., Booth, R.J.: Linguistic inquiry and word count: LIWC 2001. Mahway: Lawrence Erlbaum Associates, 71 (2001)
13. Pentheny, J.R.: The influence of movie reviews on consumers. Honors Theses and Capstones, vol. 265 (2015). https://scholars.unh.edu/honors/265
14. Reddy, S., Swaminathan, V., Motley, C.: Exploring the determinants of broadway show success. J. Market. Res. **35**(3) (1998). https://doi.org/10.2307/3152034
15. Wang, F., Liu, X., Fang, E.: User reviews variance, critic reviews variance, and product sales: an exploration of customer breadth and depth effects. J. Retail. **91**(3), 372–389 (2015)
16. Waters, L., et al.: Positive psychology in a pandemic: buffering, bolstering, and building mental health. J. Positive Psychol. (2020)
17. WHO Timeline: WHO's COVID-19 response (2021). https://www.who.int/emergencies/diseases/novel-coronavirus-2019/interactive-timeline?gclid=CjwKCAjw3MSHBhB3EiwAxcaEu7on4AXFyHOVWlHVJl0XUuGpYynP82wPfJB0pDvrKbjJGWYCzb1zvBoCIfYQAvD_BwE#event-42. Accessed 16 July 2021
18. Yarrington, J.S., et al.: Impact of the COVID-19 pandemic on mental health among 157,213 Americans. J. Affect. Disord. **286**, 64–70 (2021). https://doi.org/10.1016/j.jad.2021.02.056

E-commerce and Social Media

A Study Investigating Factors Affecting User Ratings in Mobile Games

Smriti Srivastava(✉) and Dan J. Kim

University of North Texas, Denton, TX 76203, USA
smritisrivastava@my.unt.edu, dan.kim@unt.edu

Abstract. Mobile applications have become popular in the world, and they are widely used for a variety of purposes, including entertainment, games, education, etc. Mobile gaming applications are the most popular apps on the App Store. This study analyses the relationship between different game characteristics and user ratings using signaling theory which helps app developers in designing their gaming apps. This study will determine the role of the price as well as in-app purchases of the mobile game in influencing the user rating of a mobile gaming application which can ultimately affect the success of the game. The results of the study can help developers plan their monetization strategy when they release a new game in the market.

Keywords: Signaling theory · Mobile games · In-app purchases

1 Introduction

Ralph Baer, an engineer, developed a series of prototype systems between 1966 and 1969 that sent a video signal to a television set to produce spots on the screen that could be controlled by the players. The system, which was originally able to produce only two spots, was improved in November 1967 to generate the third spot for use in a table tennis game; each player controlled a single spot that served as a paddle and struck the third spot, which acted as a ball. Little would have he known at that time that the world in which he was venturing would become a 138-billion-dollar industry in less than 50 years. The video game industry has earned more money than Hollywood and the music industry combined every year for the past 10 years. It is an ever-changing market where competition is intense, but the audience's desire is never satisfied (Ghose and Han 2014).

To say that the gaming industry is growing would be a massive understatement. It is an industry that has an upward trajectory, and Year-on-year growth is 10%. Analysts have predicted the worldwide gaming revenue to cross the 200-billion-dollar mark by 2022 (Statistica.com). 59% of Americans regularly play video games. (Statistica.com).

Mobile phone penetration as a share of the population has been on a continuous rise globally year which means that every person with a mobile phone is provided with a chance to become a gamer. According to mobile gaming statistics, games rule the app world and account for 43% of all smartphone use. 21% of Android and 25% of the iOS

© Springer Nature Switzerland AG 2022
S. Fan et al. (Eds.): WeB 2021, LNBIP 443, pp. 57–66, 2022.
https://doi.org/10.1007/978-3-031-04126-6_5

apps are games. Every fourth app downloaded from iOS and every fifth app downloaded from Android is a gaming app. (Statistica.com). People are purchasing numerous mobile options for video games. The mobile video game market is booming thanks to lengthy commutes and ease of accessibility of mobile games leading to them becoming a popular source of quick entertainment.

Mobile gaming applications can be downloaded for free or for a price paid upfront before downloading. Some consumers prefer to download the free version before paying for the full version of the game. Thus, freemium has become extremely popular today. Paid apps are not the only way for developers to make money. Developers can generate revenue through microtransactions as well (Ghose and Han 2014). Although paid apps were in the majority in the early days of the iOS App Store, today, only a small percentage of apps are paid. Users are accustomed to free apps monetized through ads or in-app purchases, so charging an upfront price can be a barrier to growth (Roshan et al. 2014). While paid apps have hurdles to overcome in achieving growth, they can still be successful when demonstrating value to customers. Nintendo released Super Mario Run for $9.99 on mobile devices. The mobile game generated $60 million in revenues despite some complaints about the high price.

Mobile game-related analytics can help the developers design games that attract more users and hence generate more revenue. Several measures of success for mobile apps have been studied by researchers, including volume of download (e.g., Liu et al. 2014), revenue, and average star rating by users (e.g., Liu et al. 2014). Song et al. (2013) found that there is a positive relationship between user ratings and the number of ratings with download volume. So, if the user ratings for an app are higher, it is more likely to be downloaded by a larger number of users compared to apps with lower user ratings.

Although the success factors for a mobile app have been studied in academics, and a positive relationship between user ratings and success of the application has been established (Lee and Raghu 2011), there is no study regarding the user ratings of mobile games and what factors influence it to the best of our knowledge.

While many previous studies estimate the valence of online reviews on sales in different product categories (Li 2018), including books, little work explores how the average review ratings for gaming apps are affected. The objectives of this study are: i) to explore user ratings and their importance in the context of mobile gaming apps, ii) to identify factors including the price of games that influence user ratings of a mobile game and to see if there is a relationship between a particular factor and user rating for mobile games, iii) to adopt a new user rating mechanism, Aggregated User-perceived Rating (AUR) (Ali et al. 2017) and test whether it is a better approach to explain the success of games, and ultimately iv) to provide theoretical and practical implications that can help mobile developers and academia.

2 Literature Review

2.1 User Rating and Importance

With the rise of the internet, the consumer information market has changed drastically. Most websites have space where users can give their reviews and rate the service or product. All apps can be rated and reviewed by users on the app market. Consequently, the sale of products and services is now largely being driven by user ratings (Chevalier and Mayzlin 2006; Chintagunta et al. 2010; Moe et al. 2011). The spread of user ratings is considered a positive development for consumer welfare by most people. Due to these user ratings, consumers are supposedly becoming more rational decision-makers, making objectively better choices, and becoming less susceptible to the influence of marketing and branding (de Langhe et al. 2015). The literature on the effects of online word-of-mouth (WOM) or user reviews has been rapidly growing during the last ten years. Researchers have also explored the connection between consumer ratings and sales in the context of markets such as beer, DVD, and video games (Clemons et al. 2006, Zhu and Zhang 2010).

It would be difficult for users to know which games they would like the most with so many gaming applications available at their fingertips. One option is for them to download and try a variety of games to determine which one is the best. This, however, would be impractical due to a large number of apps. Users will be best served by reviewing app ratings and reviews. When one views an app in the app store, one can see its ratings and feedback. Gaming apps are rated on a scale of one to five stars, with the overall average rating displayed on the app page and in search results. App reviews are user feedback that typically describes their personal interactions with the app, such as what they like most about it, problems, or suggestions for improvement. Ratings and reviews are essential for an app's success due to the following three reasons.

First and foremost, app visibility is determined by ratings and feedback. It would be more difficult for potential users to discover an app that does not have enough ratings and feedback. This is primarily because the app ratings and reviews are a huge element for App Store Optimization (ASO). ASO raises the visibility of an app in app stores, increasing the likelihood of further purchases. The first few games that appear in the results are usually the most popular and have the most downloads. However, positive reviews too can help a gaming app rise to the top of search results, making it easier for people to find and trust it. Ratings and reviews greatly influence potential users to download a game, thus significantly affecting a game's success. App stores consider games with higher ratings to be more important, and therefore give them a higher ranking (Roshan et al. 2019).

The second reason why ratings and reviews are important for a gaming app's success, is that users' value fellow users' reviews before downloading a game. Not only do the reviews make the app visible, they also provide important information that can determine a user's chance of downloading a gaming app. According to an Apptentive study, 79% of consumers check ratings and reviews before downloading an app. People also use feedback and reviews as a guide while purchasing and installing. The conversion rate, or the number of users who download the app, is aided by ratings and feedback. The conversion rate, or the percentage of users who download the app, is aided by ratings and feedback. Furthermore, according to the Apptentive report, ratings and feedback affect users' decisions to download or buy an app. Users value app review so much that 96% of t hem will consider installing an app with a minimum of four-star rating (Apptentive.com).

Finally, the third reason why ratings and reviews are crucial is that users like to point out their grievances and complaints in-app reviews, such as bugs and certain app features they dislike (or have issues with) along with shortcomings on app performance. Negative experiences tend to encourage more users to leave a rating or review, which detracts from the positive ones. According to Apptentive's report, 65% of app users leave reviews when they are dissatisfied with the app's features, but only 49% leave reviews for satisfactory services. High ratings and positive feedback commend the apps, but lapses are inevitable, highlighting the role of negative feedback. Ratings and feedback will reveal problems with the apps, and the developers' initiative in developing solutions and improvements is rewarded (Roshan et al. 2018).

2.2 App Monetization Strategies

In-app Purchases. A popular app monetization strategy is in-app purchases or IAP. In this strategy, the app itself, along with some of the basic features of the app, is free. This gives the app developer to let the user taste a miniature version of the app. If the user finds the game interesting in the demo form and would like to explore the advanced versions with premium features (say getting extra lives), then she will have to pay for it.

In some situations, customers can still get access to premium features without paying anything. If they are patient enough to wait for certain features to be unlocked or to engage with the app frequently enough, then they can use the app for free indefinitely. In other situations, such choices won't be available, and only a certain number of things would be made available for free by developers, and others only obtainable through in-app purchases (Roshan et al. 2014).

In-app Advertising. In-app advertising or IAD is a popular monetization strategy, in which app developers get paid to show advertisements within their mobile app. Not only do apps drive mobile usage, but they also drive global media consumption. Thus, in-app advertising is an important marketing channel for brands and companies.

Mobile devices, unlike desktop or laptop computers, are more often only used by one person. This means that the apps on a particular device are closely connected to the personal life and daily habits of its owner. This also makes the in-app environment an ideal place for advertisers to create effective and personal advertising touchpoints (Roshan et al. 2014).

Pay to Download Upfront (Paid Download). Charging an upfront price to download an app is the oldest app monetization strategy. The game developers just set a price and collect the money after the app store of choice takes its cut. In the early days of the iOS App Store, the majority of the apps were paid apps with an upfront download cost. There wasn't any structure to monetize apps through advertisements or in-app purchases in 2008. With time, the number of app developers on the market increased drastically and user expectations changed. Only a small percentage of apps have an upfront download cost today. Users are accustomed to free apps that are monetized through ads or in-app purchases, so charging an upfront price can be a barrier to growth (Roshan et al. 2014).

While paid apps have hurdles to overcome in achieving growth, they can still be successful when they clearly demonstrate value to customers. Nintendo released Super Mario Run for $9.99 on mobile devices. Despite some complaints about the high price, the mobile game generated $60 million in revenues.

Subscription Purchased via the App Store. Subscriptions are a subclass of in-app purchases. While standard in-app purchases are typically consumable, meaning they are paid for on a per-use basis, subscriptions can bring in steady recurring revenue. The game company decides the subscription model, such as monthly or yearly, and then the money consistently rolls in once customers are acquired. Providing value is the key to gaining those loyal, paying customers. When done correctly, putting certain features and information behind a paywall can be highly beneficial. After all, a freemium model helped turn Netflix, a video streaming service, into a multibillion-dollar corporation. In terms of success, Netflix is a unicorn, but apps of all sizes may benefit from a freemium subscription-based income model. For example, if paying a subscription means removing adverts from the app, devoted customers may be willing to pay. Users who aren't as interested in paying a subscription fee can still be monetized through in-app advertising. Charging the right amount and delivering value can make a subscription-based monetization strategy a success (Roshan et al. 2014).

2.3 Signaling Theory

The signaling theory has been studied extensively in the literature and has been used to examine how customers assess product quality when presented with material (Wells et al. 2011). The theory consists of these elements: signals, asymmetries of information, signal credibility, and signal outcomes. A signal is a piece of information that is extrinsic to the product that a seller can use to inform the buyer. Some signals used in prior literature are price, brand, warranty, etc. Asymmetry of information occurs because there is a lack of information about the product before purchasing, which changes to clarity once the consumer has bought the product and can use it to assess its quality and features. When a seller's capital or reputation is at stake if they transmit a misleading signal and offer a low-quality product, the signal is said to be credible (Wells et al. 2011). The signal outcome is generally reduced asymmetry of information about the product according to past literature, which in turn affects the purchase intention (Wells et al. 2011).

2.4 Prior Studies

Our paper builds on previous studies on the success of gaming applications as well as user rating literature. Carare (2012) showed the impact of today's best-seller rank information on tomorrow's demand using Apple App Store data. Garg and Telang (2013) provide a technique to calibrate the sales ranking and sales quantity relationship for apps using publicly available data from Apple App Store. The usage of an app is influenced by its structural positioning within the app network (Kim et al. 2014). The intrinsic preference and satiation levels of different app categories were quantified by Han et al. (2014). They also examine whether addiction to mobile apps is socially rational. The risk of competitors' entry impacts the timing and quality of app entry (Liu et al. 2014).

Roshan et al. (2019) examine the dynamics of success for mobile games. For greater exposure to their games, developers strive for a high ranking in ranking lists (Bergvall-Kåreborn and Howcroft 2011). Anthony et al. examined the relationship between rating, price, and popularity in the Blackberry World App Store. Apple App Store developers often collaborate with their peers who have popular apps in order to market their apps as soon as they are released.

The revenue is studied in Alomari et al. (2016) with respect to 31 attributes for 50 iPhone games. The main goal of the study is to identify the ten most important features in game development. They confirm a strong relationship between the total number of people who run or get engaged with a mobile game and its revenue. The top 10 features are Invite friends feature, Skill tree, Leaderboard, Unlock content, Soft currency, Facebook, Customizable, Event offer, Request friend help, Time skips. Offering free applications, higher initial popularity, investment in less common categories, continuous updates on app features and price, and higher user reviews on Apps are all linked to higher sales performance, according to Lee and Raghu (2014). Selecting a less competitive genre for an application and maintaining the application's quality at higher levels by frequently updating the application was shown to be positively associated with the application staying among the top applications for an extended period of time.

3   Research Model and Hypotheses

Several authors have used average user rating to measure the success of a mobile application in the literature. However, the average user rating does not consider the number of reviews that the application has received. Hence, it may lead to confusing results. For example, Gmail app is rated 4.3 (average) on the Apple App store by around 250 million people, while InstAddr mail app has an average rating of 4.7 but only 235 ratings. Although Gmail app has a lower rating, it is still perceived to be the better app and most users would prefer to download that over InstAddr. Hence, we use an aggregated variable called Aggregated User-perceived Rating (AUR) as the dependent variable. (Ali et al. 2017).

$$\text{AUR}(\text{app}_i) = \frac{v_i \times r_i}{v_i + m} + \frac{m \times c}{v_i + m} \tag{1}$$

Where v_i is the number of ratings for app_i, r_i is the average stars for the app_i, m is the average number of ratings (for all apps in the dataset), and c is the average number of stars (for all apps in the dataset).

We plan to test whether AUR is a better variable than Average user ratings in the gaming context. The test results can be helpful for practitioners and academics for future research to get better results for their model. The app developers not only gain from the sale of the mobile game (if it is not free) but also from microtransactions. As mentioned above, in-app advertisement (IAD) and in-app purchases (IAP) are two ways developers can earn through microtransactions. The presence of IAD and IAP gives the developers an incentive to lower the game price. Hence, it is likely that IAP and IAD affect the AUR.

IAP and IAD are not the only factors that can affect AUR. Size may also affect the user ratings. Extremely large gaming apps that occupy more memory may take longer to download on a device. They are also more likely to crash if the mobile device does not have enough processing memory. This can affect the user ratings of the game. On the other hand, if the game is too small in size, it may not be able to support high-quality animation and hence may not be liked by consumers as much as more sophisticated higher quality games. Languages can also affect user ratings. Multilingual gaming apps are more likely to have higher AUR due to their reach to a wider audience. Also, as the number of consumers downloading a game increases, it is likely that the AUR will also increase. Hence, the number of downloads for a given mobile gaming application can affect user ratings.

3.1 Model

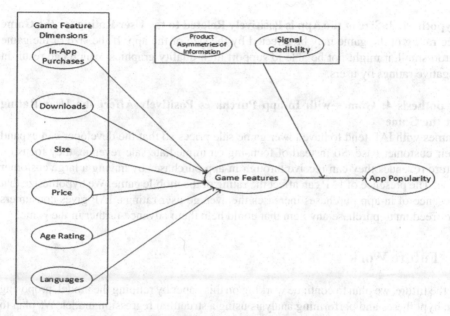

Fig. 1 Proposed research model

3.2 Hypotheses

Hypothesis 1: Multilingual Feature in the Gaming Application is Positively Associated with User Rating

If a game supports multiple languages, then it is likely to have a wider audience. This may increase the number of downloads of the game. Since people can play the game in their native language, they are more likely to download the game and give it a higher user rating compared to a game that only supports one language which may not be the native language for many people.

Hypothesis 2: There is no Linear Relationship between the Price and the Rating of Game

Most of the games on the App Store or Google Play are free. Some games can be downloaded for small prices (e.g., $1.99 or $2.99), while others may cost as high as $60. Consumers may have different expectations from the game based on the price of the game. If the mobile game is free but has great features, the user might rate the mobile game positively. On the other hand, the game might not be free and if the user is not satisfied with the app, they may be tempted to rate the app negatively.

We hypothesize that when the price of the game increases but is still low, the average user ratings increase until a certain price and then the user ratings start decreasing.

Hypothesis 3: Size of the App is Positively Related to the User Rating for the Game

The rating of the game may be affected by the size of the app. If the size of the game is too small, it might not be able to support high-quality graphics, which can result in negative ratings by users.

Hypothesis 4: Games with In-app Purchases Positively Affect the User Rating for the Game

Games with IAP tend to have lower game sale prices so that the developer can expand their customer base. So instead of focusing on immediate sale revenue, they focus on future revenues they can receive through in-app purchases by having a large customer base. The presence of IAP can affect the rating of the mobile game. We hypothesize that presence of in-app purchases increases the average user ratings. IAP gives consumers the freedom to purchase any item that could help them advance further in the game.

4 Future Work

In the future, we plan to continue working on this paper by refining the model, proposing the hypotheses and performing analysis using a structural regression model. We plan to use a data set that was collected from Apple App Store from the US Market in August 2019 (Tristan 2019). The complete dataset consists of 17,000 apps. We also plan to use data from Google Play Store in this study. The dataset we used includes 7548 gaming apps from the Apple app store. The dataset has been cleaned, and some variables were extracted which include AUR and the number of games by a particular developer.

Future work will involve using two datasets of games, one from the Apple Store and one from Google Play, to perform analysis as per our proposed model. We plan to look for additional factors that can improve our model as well as collect data according to the factors included in the model. Additionally, an analysis will be done to compare the difference between AUR and average user ratings to determine which variable is better in determining the success of the mobile gaming application. Robustness checks will also be done in the future.

5 Potential Contributions

The potential contributions in the future of the completed research paper are mentioned in this section. We plan to determine the role of the price as well as in-app purchases of the mobile game in influencing the user rating of a mobile gaming application which can ultimately affect the success of the game. This can help developers plan their monetization strategy when they release a new game in the market. We plan to examine all the factors that influence user ratings of a mobile game to see if there is a relationship between a particular factor and user rating for mobile games. This can also help mobile game developers as they design their new games. We will test Aggregated User-perceived Rating (AUR) (Ali et al. 2017) in the context of mobile games to see if it is a better variable to explain the success of games which can be helpful for mobile developers as well as academia in their future research.

The theoretical model to explain what features of a mobile game influence user ratings of mobile games will add to the growing literature on mobile games and mobile analytics. Such a model will also benefit the mobile developers and managers in creating their brand's market strategy and optimizing gaming app content and features as they release their game on the app market. Further, we plan to investigate the differences between customer rating behavior towards games on Apple Store versus Google Play. This can help mobile game developers to tailor their strategies according to the platform.

References

Ali, M., Joorabchi, M.E., Mesbah, A.: Same app, different app stores: a comparative study. In: Proceedings - 2017 IEEE/ACM 4th International Conference on Mobile Software Engineering and Systems, MOBILESoft 2017 (2017). https://doi.org/10.1109/MOBILESoft.2017.3

Alomari, K.M., Soomro, T.R., Shaalan, K.: Mobile gaming trends and revenue models. In: Fujita, H., Ali, M., Selamat, A., Sasaki, J., Kurematsu, M. (eds.) Trends in Applied Knowledge-Based Systems and Data Science. IEA/AIE 2016. Lecture Notes in Computer Science, vol. 9799, pp. 671–683 Springer, Cham (2016). https://doi.org/10.1007/978-3-319-42007-3_58

Bergvall-Kåreborn, B., Howcroft, D.: Mobile applications development on apple and google platforms, communications of the association for information systems (2011). https://doi.org/10.17705/1cais.02930

Carare, O.: The impact of bestseller rank on demand: evidence from the app market. Int. Econ. Rev. (2012). https://doi.org/10.1111/j.1468-2354.2012.00698.x

Chevalier, J.A., Mayzlin, D.: The effect of word of mouth on sales: online book reviews. J. Market. Res. (2006). https://doi.org/10.1509/jmkr.43.3.345

Chintagunta, P.K., Gopinath, S., Venkataraman, S.: The effects of online user reviews on movie box office performance: accounting for sequential rollout and aggregation across local markets. Market. Sci. (2010). https://doi.org/10.1287/mksc.1100.0572

Clemons, E.K., Gao, G., Hitt, L.M.: When online reviews meet hyperdifferentiation: a study of the craft beer industry. J. Manag. Inf. Syst. (2006). https://doi.org/10.2753/MIS0742-1222230207

Garg, R., Telang, R.: Inferring app demand from publicly available data. MIS Q. Manag. Inf. Syst. (2013). (https://doi.org/10.25300/MISQ/2013/37.4.12).

Ghose, A., Han, S.P.: Estimating demand for mobile applications in the new economy. Manag. Sci. (2014). https://doi.org/10.1287/mnsc.2014.1945

Han, S.P., Park, S., Oh, W.: An empirical analysis of consumption patterns for mobile apps and web: a multiple discrete-continuous extreme value approach. In: 35th International Conference on Information Systems Building a Better World Through Information Systems, ICIS 2014 (2014)

Lee, G., Raghu, T.S.: Determinants of mobile apps success: evidence from the app store market. J. Manag. Inf. Syst. (2014). https://doi.org/10.2753/MIS0742-1222310206

Lee, G., Raghu, T.S.: Product portfolio and mobile apps success: evidence from app store market. In: 17th Americas Conference on Information Systems 2011, AMCIS 2011 (2011)

Li, X.: Impact of average rating on social media endorsement: the moderating role of rating dispersion and discount threshold. Inf. Syst. Res. (2018). https://doi.org/10.1287/isre.2017.0728

Liu, C.Z., Au, Y.A., Choi, H.S.: Effects of freemium strategy in the mobile app market: an empirical study of google play. J. Manag. Inf. Syst. (2014). https://doi.org/10.1080/07421222.2014.995564

Moe, W.W., Trusov, M., Smith, R.H.: The value of social dynamics in online product ratings forums. J. Market. Res. (2011). https://doi.org/10.1509/jmkr.48.3.444

Roshan Kokabha, M., Tuunainen, V., Hekkala, R.: How mobile game startups excel in the market. In: Proceedings of the 52nd Hawaii International Conference on System Sciences (2019). https://doi.org/10.24251/hicss.2019.650

Roshan, M., Hekkala, R., Tuunainen, V.K.: Utilization of accelerator facilities in mobile app developer startups. In: 26th European Conference on Information Systems: Beyond Digitization - Facets of Socio-Technical Change, ECIS 2018 (2018)

Song, C., Park, K., Kim, B.C.: Impact of online reviews on mobile app sales: open versus closed platform comparison. In: Proceedings - Pacific Asia Conference on Information Systems, PACIS 2013 (2013)

Tristan (2019). https://www.kaggle.com/tristan581/17k-apple-app-store-strategy-games

Wells, J., Valacich, J., Hess, T.: What signal are you sending? How website quality influences perceptions of product quality and purchase intentions. MIS Q. **35**, 373–396 (2011). https://doi.org/10.2307/23044048

Zhu, F., Zhang, X.: Impact of online consumer reviews on sales: the moderating role of product and consumer characteristics. J. Market. (2010). https://doi.org/10.1509/jmkg.74.2.133

An Insight into Social Media Continuance Use: Through Systematic Literature Review

Debalina Bera[✉] and Dan J. Kim

University of North Texas, 1155 Union Cir, Denton, TX 7620, USA
`debalina.bera@unt.edu`

Abstract. This study investigates social media's continuous use through a systematic literature review. Through the theoretical lens of the chronological stage model, the study proposes a research model and will empirically validate the continuous and increasing use of social media. This study is thus expected to augment our IS research community by providing theoretical explanations on the social media provided affordances. Thereby, expected to help practitioners to identify a trend of social media use, to be able to predict the future need, which we believe will drive the underlying force of social media's continuous use.

Keywords: Social media applications · Chronological stage model · Affordances · Utility themes

1 Introduction

Social media as per its functional specification is "Internet-based applications that build on the ideological and technological foundations of Web 2.0", where Web 2.0 means that "content and applications are no longer created and published by individuals but modified by users in a participatory and collaborative fashion" [15]. Social Media is ubiquitous in individuals' lives and, is increasingly being used in companies too for internal organizational use and external business use. The advance of the internet facilitates offline interactions that have been resulted in the rapid growth of virtual communities with activities ranging from the economic and marketing to the social and educational sector. These internets facilitated interactions through the electronic media; known as social media has become an inexpensive medium that enables millions of people worldwide to exchange information and knowledge. Knowledge has been advanced as the source of competitive advantage in today's world [27], often discrete [5], yet increasing closer in distance with the advent of new forms of information and communication technologies (ICTs) such as social media [15]. Social media has radically changed the scope, boundaries, and dynamics of social interactions. It affords platforms to support individual communication unrestricted by the constraints of time and space. Besides, it fosters communication, knowledge transfer, managerial power enactment in organizational setup as a vehicle for developing customer insights, accessing knowledge, co-creating ideas and concepts with users, and supporting new product launches' [26]. Thus, Communication and content access and sharing intentions are two pillars of forces of using social media by the individual, business, and organization. There are several other tasks like online gaming options, self-profiling, and product profiling which are increasingly being popular. This shows, various types of affordances being offered by social media since its inception, however, to the best of our knowledge, gratifications have mainly been used as influential factors to explain social media's continuous use behaviors. Therefore, in this study, we intend to explore social media's multiple affordances through a chronological literature review and explain its continuous use based on the identified affordances.

The aim of this empirical research with a systematic literature review is three-fold. First, we will create a chronological stage model of social media evolution to identify the corresponding utilities of social media. Secondly, we will create a research model based on the generally observed trend of utility themes, i.e., affordances or features. Next, we will validate the research model empirically. In sum, based on that chronological phase model, the conceptual research model, and level of use context, we plan to explore the social media provided affordances that explain its continuous use based on a theoretical understanding. Specific Research Questions are 1. How the utilities or social media provided affordances have chronologically evolved, and what are those utility themes? 2. And, what factors are influencing towards continuous use of social media?

2   Prior Literature Reviews and Theoretical Foundations

Two major tasks, interaction and information sharing have been widely studied as a central research construct in the area of social media [1]. Though there are several types of research on social media accumulated, only a few studies have reviewed literature about different types of social media that can provide information on specific features provided by social media. Table 1 associates those few prior studies that did focus on different types of social media. As the critical success factors about, social media have evolved with time, the chronological review can provide important insights for researchers and practitioners. Furthermore, the current study focuses on how the major affordances of different types of social media and users' utility requirements have evolved.

2.1   Types of Social Media

The typology developed here is based on social media provided features collected from IS literature on social media research. Social media are web-based applications and interactive platforms that facilitate the creation, discussion, modification, and exchange of user-generated content [15, 19]. In a broad sense, social media refers to a conversational, distributed mode of content generation, dissemination, and communication among communities [28]. Social media are therefore not limited to social networks like Facebook but includes several other applications like blogs, business networks, collaborative projects, enterprise social networks, forums, microblogs, photo sharing, product/services reviews, social bookmarking, social gaming, video sharing, and virtual worlds.

Table 1. Previous IS literature on general social media applications.

Authors (year)	Focus	Previous articles
Ngai et al. (2015)	Theories used research constructs, and developed conceptual frameworks in their studies, a systematic and structured literature review based on five leading online academic databases were conducted	46 articles from 5 IS journals
Karahanna et al. (2018)	Develops a need–affordances–features (NAF) perspective on social media use	Not specified
Simeon et al. (2011)	History of social media	Not specified
Kaplan and Haenlein. (2010)	Difference between Web 2.0 and social media by considering 6 types of social media applications which are collaborative projects, blogs, content communities, social networking sites, virtual game worlds, and virtual social worlds	Not specified

2.2 Features

The concept of feature/affordance originates from ecological psychology literature; it represents the notion of "opportunities for action" as perceived by an organism in its environment [13]. The original conceptualization of affordance simultaneously considers the features of an object (e.g., interactivity feature of social media) and a perceiving entity (e.g., an individual).

2.3 Theoretical Background on Motivation to Use

Self-Determination Theory or SDT posits that there are two main types of motivation—intrinsic and extrinsic that explain an individual's volitional and non-volitional activities [10]). Intrinsic motivation takes people doing an activity because they find it interesting and derive spontaneous satisfaction from the activity itself. Extrinsic motivation, in contrast, needs an instrumentality between the activity and some separable consequences such as tangible or verbal rewards, so satisfaction comes not from the activity itself but rather from the extrinsic consequences to which the activity [12] (Gagné and Deci 2005). Since its inception, social media use has been progressed from requirement to volitional use. Out of six types of motivation (that includes four types of extrinsic, one intrinsic, and one amotivation), volitional motivations are intrinsic and three types of extrinsic (introjected, identified, and, integrated) motivations.

The review of the four main types of volitional motivations mentioned on social media use highlights two important points. First, previous studies demonstrated the appropriateness of the motivations in the context of social media [25]. Second, although social media continuous use motives vary among individuals, situations, and different types of social media, most previous studies on social media have dealt with the following specific motivational factors: entertainment, information/surveillance [21].

2.4 Systematic Literature Review

In selecting relevant articles to properly answer our research questions, we followed a widely accepted method for literature review called a systematic literature review, which is considered replicable, transparent, objective, unbiased, and rigorous [3]. Systematics is an attempt to understand the evolutionary interrelationships of living things, trying to interpret how life has diversified and changed over time.

2.5 Chronicle Evolution of Social Applications and Corresponding Utilities

Motivated by the above definition of systematics as in Wikipedia, we in this paper plan to look into the historical development of social media to its modern-day use, to understand how social media's use has been evolved, which we consider will give us an alternative lens to identify the influential utility factors behind social media's use intention, over time. We argue that the development of internet technologies contributes to shaping and changing the notion of and the nature of social media use. This section discusses four phases of internet eras based on below (Fig. 1.) chronological stage model of web evolution. Four chronological stages will be used later as the theoretical lenses for this literature review. There is no well-established stage model for the advancement of web technologies related to social media evolution in the academic literature. However, [11] provides useful insights.

Based on Fig. 1., we developed Table 2. It provides the trend of utilities that has evolved; we can infer that first people were more goal-oriented when they tried to collect information, news, etc., using paper-based media, telephone, radio, email communication, and then they are gradually being inclined towards being emotion-driven, self-expressive and fun-oriented which has been driving them to use the social media's networking sites for tightening personal interactions, profile making apps to express individualistic specialty and virtual gaming apps for enjoying ultimate fun feelings. The recent use of interactive social media news applications is showing the trend of people's intention towards not only collecting news or information but also analyzing those to make it useful by providing self-views, asking queries, and discussing the information's usability by interacting with fellow newsreaders about its content.

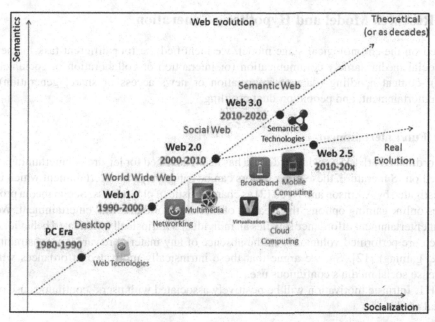

Fig. 1. Chronological stage model based on web evolution

Table 2. Chronological evolution of social media applications and corresponding utilities.

Social media evolution era	Internet/Technical specification	Social media technology/Applications	Focused utilities mentioned in is research
PC Era (1980–1990)	ARPANET, a TELENET-based system, and an e-mail only service called phone net	GDSS, Lotus notes, Email-only service called phone net	Communication
WWW 1.0 (1991–2000)	Static websites. Mostly publishing/Brochure-ware. Limited to reading only for the majority. Proprietary and closed access. Corporations mostly non-community's HTTP, HTML	Email, Use the net, IRC, Six degrees, Live journal	Long-distance communication, Article posting/Post to the news feed, File sharing/Link sharing, Social networking, Profiling, Following a friend
WWW 2.0 (2001–2010)	Publishing as well as participation, User experience, Tagging keyword search AJAX, JavaScript frameworks (jQuery, Dojo, YUI, Ext Js etc.), XML, JSON	Wikipedia, Friendster, Myspace, LinkedIn, YouTube, Facebook, Twitter, Blogging	Content creation/Sharing/Accessing, Communication/Collaboration/Interaction/Socialization, Fun/Entertainment/ Online games, Personal/Product profiling
WWW 3.0 (2011–Current)	Mostly drag and drop, Broadband, Cloud computing, Mobile computing	Microblogging	Content creation/Sharing/Accessing, Communication/Collaboration/Interaction/Socialization, Fun/Online games, Personal/Product profiling

3   Research Model and Hypothesis Generation

Based on the chronological stage model, we identified the four different task themes of social media namely communication (or interaction or collaboration or socialization), content handling (data or information or news access or share, generation), fun/entertainment, and people/product profiling.

3.1   Fun/Entertainment

According to Park [25], social media use has been identified for leisure or entertainment. Based on IS literature, these other factors can be categorized as entertainment which is investigated by Atkinson and Kydd [2] as characteristic of playfulness. Social media provides online gaming options; the creation of a virtual world provides entertainment. We posit entertainment affordance satisfies an individual's intrinsically motivated behaviors, which are performed voluntarily in the absence of any material rewards or constraints (e.g., gaming) [12]. So, we argue that these intrinsically motivated affordances will increase social media's continuous use.

H1. Intrinsic motivation will be positively associated with users' continuous use of social media.

3.2   Self-profiling

Key developmental activities such as exploring individual identity [10], social identity [23], and sense of self [18] appear to be carried out through social media and SNS such as Facebook and Instagram. We posit profiling affordance satisfies an individual's integrated motivation, which leads to voluntary behavior that is valued by the individual and is perceived as being chosen by oneself (e.g., a satisfying sense of self by creating a good profile picture) [12]. Hence, we argue, these integration-motivated affordances will increase social media's continuous use.

H2. Integrated motivation will be positively associated with users' continuous use of social media.

3.3   Content/Information/Data/News Handling

We consider social media in the broadest sense of the term and define it as an online service through which users can create and share a variety of content [4]. Other studies mentioned social media as platforms that facilitate the creation, discussion, modification, and exchange of user-generated content [15, 19]. For instance, video sharing (e.g., YouTube), blogging, microblogging (e.g., Twitter), and social networking (e.g., Facebook or hosted online communities) are used for content handling to share with customers, external partners, or suppliers [7, 8]. This creates the idea of the motivation behind social media's use for the exchange of content or information or generating content. We posit this content-handling affordance satisfies an individual's identified motivation which results in performing a voluntary activity that is ego and goal-oriented (e.g., user-generated content that reflects a user's opinion on a certain topic) [12]. So, we argue that the identification motivated affordances will increase social media's continuous use.

H3. Identified motivation will be positively associated with users' continuous use of social media.

3.4 Content/Information/Data/News Handling

By providing users with a public space in which they can interact with others (Rowe 2015a, 2015b). Other studies mentioned social media for socializing and experiencing a sense of community and staying in touch with friends [20]. Workplace communication among individuals [22]. We posit communication/interaction affordance satisfies an individual's introjected motivation, which results in performing a voluntary activity that is goal, outcome, and value-oriented (e.g., a user receiving answers from a colleague) [12]. So, we argue that introjection motivated affordances will increase social media's continuous use.

H4. Introjected motivation will be positively associated with users' continuous use of social media.

3.5 Conceptual Framework

So, we can justifiably posit that these are the four major utility themes. From the Chronological stage model, we discussed the features of different social media applications. From this descriptive position, drawing from SDT, we propose the below research model (Fig. 2.) that can provide us an insight into social media's continuance use phenomenon.

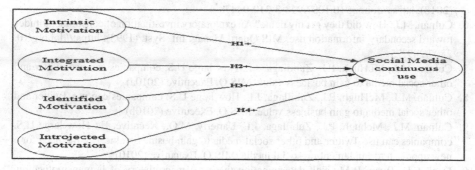

Fig. 2. Research model.

3.6 Proposed Research Method

To validate the social media's continuous use based on the chronological stage model, the study will design a web-based survey method and will validate it using PLS-SEM.

4   Conclusion

This study aims to explore social media's continuous use through a systematic literature review. Through the theoretical lens of the chronological stage model, the study proposed a research model and would empirically validate the continuous and increasing use of social media. This study is thus expected to augment our IS research community by providing theoretical explanations on social media's continuous use. Additionally, it is expected to help practitioners to identify a trend of social media affordances to be used, to be able to predict the future need.

References

1. Asur, S., Huberman, B.A.: Predicting the future with social media. In: Proceedings - 2010 IEEE/WIC/ACM International Conference on Web Intelligence, WI 2010 (2010). https://doi.org/10.1109/WI-IAT.2010.63
2. Atkinson, M.A., Kydd, C.: Individual characteristics associated with World Wide Web use empirical study of playfulness and motivation, data base for advances in information systems (1997). https://doi.org/10.1145/264701.264705
3. Boell, S.K., Cecez-Kecmanovic, D.: On being systematic in literature reviews. In: Willcocks, L.P., Sauer, C., Lacity, M.C. (eds.) Formulating Research Methods for Information Systems, pp. 48–78. Palgrave Macmillan, London (2015). https://doi.org/10.1057/9781137509888_3
4. Bolton, R.N., et al.: Understanding generation y and their use of social media: a review and research agenda. J. Serv. Manag. (2013). https://doi.org/10.1108/09564231311326987
5. Chen, S., Wang, H., Zhang, L.-J.: Blockchain – ICBC 2018. In: Proceedings blockchain-ICBC (2018). https://doi.org/10.1007/978-3-319-94478-4
6. Culnan, M.J.: How did they get my name? An exploratory investigation of consumer attitudes toward secondary information use. MIS Quart. Manag. Inf. Syst. (1993). https://doi.org/10.2307/249775
7. Culnan, M.J., McHugh, P.J., Zubillaga, J.I.: How large U.S. companies can use twitter and other social media to gain business value. MIS Q. Executive (2010a)
8. Culnan, M.J., McHugh, P.J., Zubillaga, J.I.: How large U.S. companies can use Twitter and other social media to gain business value. MIS Q. Executive (2010b)
9. Culnan, M.J., Mchugh, P.J., Zubillaga, J.I., Uarterly, M.Q., Xecutive, E.: How large U.S. companies can use Twitter and other social media to gain business value 1, 2 the need for a new approach to implementing social media. MIS Q. Executive (2010)
10. Deci, E.L., Ryan, R.M.: Self-determination theory: a macrotheory of human motivation, development, and health. Can. Psychol. (2008). https://doi.org/10.1037/a0012801
11. Edosomwan, S., Prakasan, S. K., Kouame, D., Watson, J., Seymour, T.: The history of social media and its impact on business. Management (2011)
12. Gagné, M., Deci, E.L.: Self-determination theory and work motivation. J. Organ. Behav. (2005). https://doi.org/10.1002/job.322
13. Gibson, J.J.: The Theory of Affordances (1979). In: The People, Place, and Space Reader (2014). https://doi.org/10.4324/9781315816852
14. Grasmuck, S., Martin, J., Zhao, S.: Ethno-racial identity displays on Facebook. J. Comput. Mediat. Commun. (2009). https://doi.org/10.1111/j.1083-6101.2009.01498.x
15. Kaplan, A.M., Haenlein, M., Kaplan, A.M., Haenlein, M.: Users of the world, unite! The challenges and opportunities of social media. Bus. Horiz. (2010a). https://doi.org/10.1109/WCNC.2006.1683604

16. Kaplan, A.M., Haenlein, M.: Users of the world, unite! The challenges and opportunities of social media. Bus. Horiz. (2010b). https://doi.org/10.1016/j.bushor.2009.09.003
17. Karahanna, E., Xu, S. X., Xu, Y., Zhang, N.: The needs-affordances-features perspective for the use of social media. MIS Q. Manage. Inf. Syst. (2018). https://doi.org/10.25300/MISQ/2018/11492
18. Karl, K., Peluchette, J., Schlaegel, C.: Who's posting Facebook faux pas? A cross-cultural examination of personality differences. Int. J. Sel. Assess. (2010). https://doi.org/10.1111/j.1468-2389.2010.00499.x
19. Kietzmann, J.H., Hermkens, K., McCarthy, I.P., Silvestre, B.S.: Social media? Get serious! Understanding the functional building blocks of social media. Bus. Horiz. (2011). https://doi.org/10.1016/j.bushor.2011.01.005
20. Lenhart, A., Madden, M., Macgill, A.R., Manager, P., Smith, A.: Teens and social media gains a greater foothold in teen life as they embrace the conversational nature of interactive online media. Pew Internet Am. Life Project (2007). https://doi.org/5
21. Lee, A.S.: Electronic mail as a medium for rich communication: an empirical investigation using hermeneutic interpretation. MIS Q. Manag. Inf. Syst. (1994). https://doi.org/10.2307/249762
22. Leonardi, P.M.: Ambient awareness and knowledge acquisition: using social media to learn who knows what and who knows whom. MIS Q. Manag. Inf. Syst. (2015). https://doi.org/10.25300/MISQ/2015/39.4.1
23. Manago, A.M., Graham, M.B., Greenfield, P.M., Salimkhan, G.: Self-presentation and gender on MySpace. J. Appl. Dev. Psychol. (2008). https://doi.org/10.1016/j.appdev.2008.07.001
24. Ngai, E.W.T., Tao, S.S.C., Moon, K.K.L.: Social media research: theories, constructs, and conceptual frameworks. Int. J. Inf. Manag. (2015). https://doi.org/10.1016/j.ijinfomgt.2014.09.004
25. Park, N., Kee, K.F., Valenzuela, S.: Being immersed in social networking environment: Facebook groups, uses and gratifications, and social outcomes. Cyberpsychol. Behav. (2015). https://doi.org/10.1089/cpb.2009.0003
26. Roberts, D.L., Piller, F.T., Lüttgens, D.: Mapping the impact of social media for innovation: the role of social media in explaining innovation performance in the PDMA comparative performance assessment study. J. Product Innov. Manag. (2016). https://doi.org/10.1111/jpim.12341
27. Solima, L., Della Peruta, M.R., Maggioni, V.: Managing adaptive orientation systems for museum visitors from an IoT perspective. Bus. Process Manag. J. (2016). https://doi.org/10.1108/BPMJ-08-2015-0115
28. Zeng, D., Chen, H., Lusch, R., Li, S.H.: Social media analytics and intelligence. IEEE Intell. Syst. (2010). https://doi.org/10.1109/MIS.2010.151

An Empirical Study of Brand Concept Recall as a Predictor of Brand Loyalty for Dyson

Takumi Kato[⊠] [iD]

Saitama University, 255 Shimo-Okubo, Sakura-ku, Saitama 338-8570, Japan
takumikato@mail.saitama-u.ac.jp

Abstract. Brand loyalty factors are generally explained by product/service features like design and usability. However, consumers may be attracted to superficial functionality and design, but easily switch brands when another company's product/service with higher functionality and a more fashionable design appears. If a consumer remains loyal to a brand, it is because they understand, sympathize with, and value the brand's concept. Accordingly, the present study hypothesized that consumers who recall a brand concept are more likely to exhibit loyalty than consumers who recall specific features, such as design. From the results of an online survey of consumers with Dyson vacuum cleaners in the Japanese market, the factors of brand loyalty were evaluated using structural equation modeling. As a result, no significant effect was confirmed for the design, which is generally claimed to be highly evaluated in this brand. In contrast, the brand concept claimed in this study was confirmed to have a significant positive effect. Companies should first reaffirm the importance of brand concepts. There are still many product/service brands that are equipped with functions and designs, while the brand concept remains ambiguous. Hence, the concept recall index should be emphasized in brand management.

Keywords: Brand management · Concept · Product design · Vacuum cleaner

1 Introduction

Functional values correspond to performance and durability, which can be objectively evaluated based on physical indicators. Emotional value corresponds to the design and customer experience that consumers feel subjectively. In other words, emotional value can be very high for some people, but low for others. Recently, competitiveness has shifted to emotional value rather than functional value [1]. This recognition has become widespread, and more companies are focusing on emotional values. However, even when the design is improved, a product/service can seem similar to another from the consumer's point of view, and it is difficult to increase customers' perceptions of value. One reason may be that the brand concept of the product/service (hereinafter the brand concept) is ambiguous and focuses too strongly on design/user experience (UX). Consumers may be attracted to superficial functionality and design, but they may easily switch brands when another company's product/service with higher functionality and a more fashionable

© Springer Nature Switzerland AG 2022
S. Fan et al. (Eds.): WeB 2021, LNBIP 443, pp. 76–86, 2022.
https://doi.org/10.1007/978-3-031-04126-6_7

design appears. If a consumer remains loyal to a brand, it is because they understand, sympathize with, and value the brand's concept [2].

The problem awareness, which was the starting point of this research, is placed in the field where the concept is neglected in brand management. Brand loyalty factors are generally explained by product/service features, such as performance [3, 4], quality [5, 6], design [7, 8], and UX [9, 10]. Alternatively, factor evaluation based on brand image [11], brand reputation [12, 13], word of mouth [14–16], brand trust [17, 18], and brand familiarity [19] are common. In this way, although many loyalty factors have been reported in academic research on marketing, there are very few examples of the brand concept of a product/service.

Accordingly, the present study hypothesizes that consumers who recall a brand concept are more likely to exhibit loyalty than consumers who recall specific features like design. The conditions for selecting the target product are as follows: (1) products are developed and sold under the same brand concept consistently over the long term, (2) products with functional value and emotional value, and (3) products with clear concepts that build a strong brand in the market. Therefore, the focus was on vacuum cleaners among durable consumer goods, and Dyson's product, which has the clearest brand concept, was targeted. Based on this concept, Dyson built a strong brand by equipping products with core values [20, 21]. From the results of an online survey of consumers with Dyson vacuum cleaners in the Japanese market, the factors of brand loyalty were evaluated using structural equation modeling. Although the importance of concepts is recognized as a theory of business administration and marketing, few studies have demonstrated it as a factor that explains consumer loyalty. This research shows the importance of the brand concept based on quantitative proof, and provides an opportunity to reconsider its importance in both business and academic research. Note that in this paper, brand refers to a product/service brand.

2 Literature Review and Derivation of Hypothesis

The term "brand concept" refers to brand-unique abstract meanings that typically originate from a firm's efforts to differentiate itself from its competitors [22]. A brand concept defines the value provided to customers and should meet consumers' needs [23]. The framework of a concept comprises the target (who), value and positioning (what), and execution method (how) [24, 25]. For example, Starbucks describes its concept as the "third place," for which the "who" would be consumers looking for a place to relax when they go out, the "what" is a place outside of home or work where people can relax alone or gather for a sense of community, and the "how" is by providing an atmosphere that incorporates aspects such as earth tones, comfortable music, and coffee [26]. Dyson's vacuum cleaner describes its concept as "the cleaner that doesn't lose suction," for which the "who" would be consumers dissatisfied with reduced suction, the "what" is a vacuum cleaner that does not lose suction power, and the "how" is by providing the cyclone technology without a paper bag that causes clogging [27]. Consumers then develop attitudes toward a brand through their experience with its products/services and advertising, and will be formed as brand knowledge [28, 29]. Brand image refers to consumers' cultivated perceptions of products and advertisements that are developed based on concepts devised by marketers [30]. The brand concept is the root of a product/service and has a significant impact on customer behavior.

The role of the concept within the company is the criterion for decision-making in all corporate activities, such as planning, development, production, and sales [31, 32]. Product/service development involves many day-to-day decisions by various departments, and consistent standards must be applied throughout the process. If the concept is ambiguous, resources such as technology and design cannot be effectively applied, and the product/service's purpose will shift toward the trends already seen in the industry. Regardless of the resources a company has, converting them into value for consumers depends on the concept being valuable and consistently embodied. Therefore, for a product/service to become a strong brand, it is necessary to clearly define the concept before it enters the market, and maintain the concept and embodiment perceived by the consumer over its life [33]. Product/service brands made in this way, based on the brand concept, help consumers distinguish them from competitors. In addition, the concept plays a significant role in expanding a brand or forming brand alliances. The factor that distinguishes the success or failure of a brand extension is consistency within categories and concepts [34–37]. Consumers who exhibit high loyalty also have high demands for consistency [38], and the consistency of a concept is more important than its category. For instance, Breitling for Bentley, a co-brand of Swiss mechanical watchmaker Breitling and Bentley's venerable luxury car in the UK, has a low degree of product category matching but long partnership for its expressive concept matching [39].

In brand management, specific features (e.g., performance, quality, design, and UX) have been used as factors to explain loyalty. However, few studies have evaluated loyalty factors from a brand concept perspective. In corporate marketing research, consumers are generally asked about design, function, and brand image, yet they are rarely asked about the brand concept. A method for understanding brand concept from the consumer's point of view has also been proposed [40, 41]; however, no evaluation has been performed on the loyalty factor. Although some studies have divided concepts into general categories (e.g., functional, symbolic, luxurious) [42, 43], it is difficult to determine whether these methods pinpoint whether consumers understand product concepts, because the general categories are too broad.

There are three possible reasons for why few studies deal with brand concepts. First, researchers and corporate marketers believe it is difficult for consumers to evaluate concepts that cannot be experienced directly. Second, many brand concepts are ambiguous, and marketers can lose sight of their purpose because they cannot clearly identify how their products/services are meaningful to customers [44]. When the concept is ambiguous, products/services rely on trendy, superficial designs and advanced functions, and it is difficult to evaluate the brand concept. Third, even if there is a clear concept, there may not be a consistent embodiment of the product/service, and it comes across as ambiguous in the marketplace. Much effort is required to consistently embody a concept without compromise when each corporate department makes different claims; therefore, a thoroughly implemented product/service is a rare entity that can grow into a strong brand.

However, consumers may be attracted to superficial functionality and design, but they may easily switch brands when another company's product/service appears with higher functionality and a more fashionable design. It is assumed that consumers who value the brand concept rather than superficial product/service features are likely to be more loyal [45]. Whether consumers recall the brand concept when asked about the brand image greatly influences their loyalty. In other words, if consumers have brand loyalty, consumers should be able to recall the keywords in their concept when asked about the brand image. Accordingly, the following hypothesis is derived:

H1: Consumers who recall the brand concept are likely to be satisfied and loyal when asked about the brand image.

In this research, the emphasis is on brand concept. However, Dyson vacuum cleaners have long been notable because of their distinct design. Dyson has focused on developing products with designs that are more attractive than their competitors [46]. Even the technology used in the products has been designed with aesthetics in mind. In short, the dust box of the vacuum cleaner was made transparent, and the technology was designed to be observable, which made it more attractive to consumers [47, 48]. Accordingly, the following hypothesis is derived:

H2: Consumers who recall the design are likely to be satisfied and loyal when asked about the brand image.

3 Method

3.1 Survey

This study verified the above hypotheses with the Dyson Big Ball as the target brand (canister vacuum cleaner, hereafter, Dyson). An online survey was conducted in Japan from November 5 to 10, 2020. Respondents' ages (a) ranged from 20 to 59 years; they had (b) purchased a new target product brand; and (c) they used the target brand at least once a week. The survey consisted of a screening survey and a main online survey. The screening survey identified respondents who met conditions (a)–(c). Those who met these conditions were immediately routed to the main survey. The screening survey comprised the following questions: (1) gender, (2) age, (3) marital status, (4) annual household income, (5) ownership of the target brand, (6) how the product brand was purchased (new or used), and (7) frequency of use of the brand. Data were collected from 200 people who met the conditions, and their distribution is shown in Table 1.

In the main survey, the questionnaire items were as follows: satisfaction (8), preference (9), recommendation intention (10), repurchase intention (11), and brand image (12). Items (8)–(11) were rated on a 7-point Likert scale (1 = very unsatisfied, 7 = very satisfied). The mean values were: satisfaction, 4.885; preference, 5.050; recommendation intention, 4.745; and repurchase intention, 4.535. Item (12) was a pure recall question, in which an answer was freely requested without presenting options to the respondent. This is because aided recall, where the respondent picks from a set of options, introduces bias, which may lead to the overestimation of certain options. There was concern that presenting the concept as an option would encourage consumers who are not normally aware of it. By using pure recall, respondents could provide answers about a brand concept only if they understood it.

Table 1. Respondent attributes.

Item	Breakdown	Number of respondents	Percentage
Gender	Male	87	43.5%
	Female	113	56.5%
Age	20s	45	22.5%
	30s	55	27.5%
	40s	51	25.5%
	50s	49	24.5%
Marriage status	Married	130	65.0%
	Unmarried	70	35.0%
Annual household income	−4 m¥,	39	19.5%
(m¥: million yen)	4 m¥–6 m¥	37	18.5%
	6 m¥–8 m¥	44	22.0%
	8 m¥–10 m¥	29	14.5%
	10 m¥ -	51	25.5%

3.2 Verification

It should be noted that, to date, there is no established brand concept framework or evaluation method. In this study, the focus was on whether consumers could recall the concept when asked about the brand image. To avoid introducing bias, no options were presented, and the answer was provided by pure recall. Therefore, it was judged whether the keywords of Dyson's brand concept were included in the answer. The most important word, "suction" in the concept "the cleaner that doesn't lose suction" was set as the detection target. In addition, factors that occurred more than 10 times were set as detection targets. For example, a positive factor of luxury and a negative factor of noisy were observed, but they were excluded in this study because they appeared less than 10 times. As shown in Table 2, the top three words belonging to each factor were used to detect the four factors: brand, design, heavy, and expensive. Only the concept was not included in the synonyms for a strict judgment.

When the words defined in Table 2 were detected from the answer sentences to the brand image question, it was judged that the factor was mentioned. As a result, 64 out of 200 people mentioned the concept, which is the most easily recalled brand image. However, this number is just a frequency and not a contribution to brand loyalty.

Then, as shown in Table 3, the recalls of each factor were transformed into dummy variables, and subsequent analysis was conducted. As shown in Table 4, looking at the correlation matrix, the positive correlation with the largest concept is shown for all loyalty variables (Nos. 1–4). Using these variables, the hypotheses were tested using structural equation modeling. The hypothetical model is a simple structure that influences the loyalty factor consisting of preference, recommendation intention, and repurchase intention by mediating satisfaction from the factors shown in Nos. 5–9 of Table 3. The analysis was conducted in R, and the lavaan package was used for structural equation modeling.

Table 2. Target factors and the number of people mentioning each factor.

Factor	Word 1	Word 2	Word 3	Number of people who recall each factor
Concept	Suction			64
Brand	Brand	Reputation	Name value	10
Design	Design	Stylish	Fashionable	14
Heavy	Heavy	Huge	Big	25
Expensive	Expensive	Markup	High-priced	15

Table 3. Variable list and statistics.

No	Classification	Variable	Data form	Mean	SE
1	Loyalty index	Satisfaction	7-point scale	4.885	0.106
2		Preference	7-point scale	5.050	0.099
3		Recommendation	7-point scale	4.745	0.107
4		Repurchase	7-point scale	4.535	0.117
5	Factor	Concept	0/1	0.320	0.033
6	(Recall dummy)	Brand	0/1	0.050	0.015
7		Design	0/1	0.070	0.018
8		Heavy	0/1	0.125	0.023
9		Expensive	0/1	0.075	0.019

Note: SE = standard error.

Table 4. Correlation matrix.

No	Variable	1	2	3	4	5	6	7	8
1	Satisfaction								
2	Preference	0.787							
3	Recommendation	0.772	0.772						
4	Repurchase	0.710	0.728	0.721					
5	Concept	0.195	0.174	0.159	0.141				
6	Brand	0.094	0.090	0.069	0.093	0.039			
7	Design	0.021	0.018	0.007	0.042	−0.020	0.027		
8	Heavy	−0.253	−0.240	−0.207	−0.306	−0.065	−0.017	−0.044	
9	Expensive	−0.003	−0.051	−0.065	−0.058	−0.114	−0.065	−0.078	0.122

4 Results and Discussion

Figure 1 shows the results of the structural equation modeling. The indicators of the model showed high suitability, except for AGFI: CFI = 1.000, GFI = 0.973, AGFI = 0.928, SRMR = 0.025, RMSEA = 0.000. First, the positive effect of satisfaction on loyalty is confirmed. Thus, the subject of interest is a factor that affects satisfaction. Of the five factors, concept positively contributed the highest, and "heavy" negatively contributed the highest. These two factors have significant effects at the 5% level. None of the other factors had a significant effect. Hence, the model was built by focusing on two factors that showed significant effects. As shown in Fig. 2, the indicators showed higher suitability, especially for AGFI: CFI = 1.000, GFI = 0.979, AGFI = 0.946, SRMR = 0.029, RMSEA = 0.017. The same two factors (concept and heavy) again show significant results. H1 was supported, but H2 was not. At Dyson, the appeal of the design was attracting attention, but its effect was poor. On the other hand, consumers who recall brand loyalty, which is the purpose of this study, tended to show high loyalty. It was also revealed that the biggest negative image of the brand was "heavy." Since the absolute value of its contribution is much larger than the concept, it is considered a major improvement for the brand.

The following two implications are provided in this study in marketing practice. First, companies should first reaffirm the importance of brand concepts. There are still many product/service brands that are equipped with superior functions and designs, while the brand concept remains ambiguous. The consistent embodiment of the concept plays a major role in the success of the brand. Second, the concept recall index should be emphasized in brand management. In general, after measuring loyalty, efforts are made to understand the factors that contribute to loyalty by evaluating each specific feature of the product/service brand. However, satisfaction with superficial features does not represent a passion for the brand. Consumers who understand, sympathize with, and value the brand's concept exhibit stronger loyalty. Therefore, companies should evaluate whether the concept is recalled as a brand image or reason for brand loyalty. Hopefully, the index of concept recall will gain prominence not only in the industrial world, but also in the academic world that studies consumer behavior and brand management.

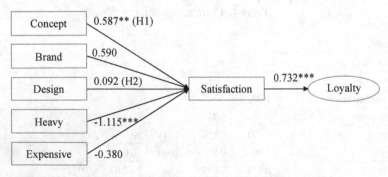

CFI : 1.000, GFI : 0.973, AGFI: 0.928, SRMR: 0.025, RMSEA : 0.000
***p<0.001; **p<0.01; *p<0.05.

Fig. 1. Results of the structural equation modeling with all factors.

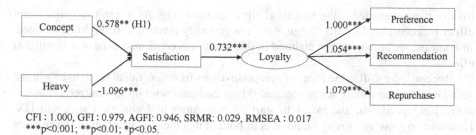

CFI : 1.000, GFI : 0.979, AGFI: 0.946, SRMR: 0.029, RMSEA : 0.017
***p<0.001; **p<0.01; *p<0.05.

Fig. 2. Results of the structural equation modeling with significant factors selected.

This study has three limitations. First, since it only covered the Japanese market, vacuum cleaners, and Dyson, the generalizability of its results remains limited. It would be desirable to broaden the scope of markets, industries, and brands in order to reach universal conclusions. In particular, the concept of Dyson vacuum cleaners is so pervasive that the concept recall rate is overwhelmingly higher than the specific features. Future research will need to include brands with lower penetration of the brand concept. Second, the results may vary depending on the evaluation method used. In this study, only the concept-related word "suction" was detected as a factor to eliminate arbitrariness. Hence, the results may vary slightly depending on the number of keywords and the questioning method (pure recall, aided recall). Third, since pure recall was applied, features that consumers usually have difficulty recalling are unlikely to appear in the evaluation (e.g., corporate social responsibility, environmental consideration). Therefore, only typical features, such as brand and design, were compared in this study. In other words, the survey method changes depending on whether the evaluation is based on factors that are easy for consumers to notice without bias or for factors that are difficult for consumers to notice despite bias. In brand management practice and research, a discussion on the method of evaluating concepts is still lacking. Further research is required on these issues.

5 Conclusion

Brand management has long been a central theme in academic research. Numerous brand loyalty factors have been reported in the past. Recently, the claim that emotional value is more effective than functional value has been conspicuous. However, before that, the perspective of brand loyalty should not be neglected. No matter how good the technology or design is, if the brand concept is ambiguous, there is a concern that they will be wasted. From the consumer's point of view, consumers with high loyalty are considered to be sympathetic to the brand concept, which is the essence of the brand.

Accordingly, the present study hypothesized that consumers who recall a brand concept are more likely to exhibit loyalty than consumers who recall specific features, such as design. The Dyson vacuum cleaner, which has a clear brand concept and is equipped with distinct designs and advanced technology, was selected as the target. This avoids overestimating the brand concept. From the results of an online survey of consumers with Dyson vacuum cleaners in the Japanese market, the factors of brand loyalty were evaluated using structural equation modeling. As a result, no significant effect was confirmed for the design, which is generally claimed to be highly evaluated. In contrast, the brand concept claimed in this study was confirmed to have a significant effect.

Recently, the shift in the focus of competitiveness from functional value to emotional value has become widely acknowledged. Many companies set up specialized organizations, hire specialists, and invest in start-up companies to focus on design and UX. However, to grow as a strong brand, it is important that the starting point of the concept is clear and valuable. If the purpose is to "use the means of design/UX" while the concept remains ambiguous, the effective means will be wasted. The importance of the brand concept has been discussed as a theory, but this study is a rare example of work that quantitatively shows its effect. This result encourages practitioners and researchers to rethink the importance of brand concepts.

Acknowledgment. This work was supported by JSPS KAKENHI Grant Number 20K22115.

References

1. Kato, T.: Synergistic effect of matching corporate and product brand images on purchase intentions: comparing the importance of functional and emotional value. J. Brand Manag. **28**(6), 671–684 (2021). https://doi.org/10.1057/s41262-021-00250-w
2. Aaker, D.A., Joachimsthaler, E.: Brand Leadership. The Free Press, New York (2000)
3. Kumar, V., Batista, L., Maull, R.: The impact of operations performance on customer loyalty. Serv. Sci. **3**(2), 158–171 (2011). https://doi.org/10.1287/serv.3.2.158
4. Yeh, C.H., Wang, Y.S., Yieh, K.: Predicting smartphone brand loyalty: consumer value and consumer-brand identification perspectives. Int. J. Inf. Manag. Sci. **36**(3), 245–257 (2016). https://doi.org/10.1016/j.ijinfomgt.2015.11.013
5. Shen, C., Yahya, Y.: The impact of service quality and price on passengers loyalty towards low-cost airlines: the Southeast Asia perspective. J. Air Transp. Manag. **91**, 101966 (2021). https://doi.org/10.1016/j.jairtraman.2020.101966
6. Zehir, C., Şahin, A., Kitapçı, H., Özşahin, M.: The effects of brand communication and service quality in building brand loyalty through brand trust; the empirical research on global brands. Proc. Soc. Behav. Sci. **24**, 1218–1231 (2011). https://doi.org/10.1016/j.sbspro.2011.09.142
7. Hsu, C.L., Chen, Y.C., Yang, T.N., Lin, W.K., Liu, Y.H.: Does product design matter? Exploring its influences in consumers psychological responses and brand loyalty. Inf. Technol. People **31**(3), 886–907 (2018). https://doi.org/10.1108/ITP-07-2017-0206
8. Kato, T.: Functional value vs emotional value: a comparative study of the values that contribute to a preference for a corporate brand. IJIM Data Insights **1**(2), 100024 (2021). https://doi.org/10.1016/j.jjimei.2021.100024
9. Chen, Y.Y.: Why do consumers go internet shopping again? Understanding the antecedents of repurchase intention. J. Organ. Comput. Electron. Commer. **22**(1), 38–63 (2012). https://doi.org/10.1080/10919392.2012.642234
10. Lee, D., Moon, J., Kim, Y.J., Mun, Y.Y.: Antecedents and consequences of mobile phone usability: linking simplicity and interactivity to satisfaction, trust, and brand loyalty. Inf. Manag. **52**(3), 295–304 (2015). https://doi.org/10.1016/j.im.2014.12.001
11. Unal, S., Aydın, H.: An investigation on the evaluation of the factors affecting brand love. Proc. Soc. Behav. Sci. **92**, 76–85 (2013). https://doi.org/10.1016/j.sbspro.2013.08.640

12. Han, S.H., Chen, C.H.S., Lee, T.J.: The interaction between individual cultural values and the cognitive and social processes of global restaurant brand equity. Int. J. Hosp. Manag. **94**, 102847 (2021). https://doi.org/10.1016/j.ijhm.2020.102847
13. Selnes, F.: An examination of the effect of product performance on brand reputation, satisfaction and loyalty. Eur. J. Mark. **27**(9), 19–35 (1993). https://doi.org/10.1108/030905693100 43179
14. Eelen, J., Özturan, P., Verlegh, P.W.: The differential impact of brand loyalty on traditional and online word of mouth: the moderating roles of self-brand connection and the desire to help the brand. Int. J. Res. Mark. **34**(4), 872–891 (2017). https://doi.org/10.1016/j.ijresmar. 2017.08.002
15. Liang, L.J., Choi, H.C., Joppe, M.: Understanding repurchase intention of Airbnb consumers: perceived authenticity, electronic word-of-mouth, and price sensitivity. J. Travel Tour. Mark. **35**(1), 73–89 (2018). https://doi.org/10.1080/10548408.2016.1224750
16. Podoshen, J.S.: Word of mouth, brand loyalty, acculturation and the American Jewish consumer. J. Consum. Mark. **23**(5), 266–282 (2006). https://doi.org/10.1108/073637606106 81664
17. Chaudhuri, A., Holbrook, M.B.: The chain of effects from brand trust and brand affect to brand performance: the role of brand loyalty. J. Mark. **65**(2), 81–93 (2001). https://doi.org/ 10.1509/jmkg.65.2.81.18255
18. Lau, G.T., Lee, S.H.: Consumers trust in a brand and the link to brand loyalty. J. Mark.-Focus. Manag. **4**(4), 341–370 (1999). https://doi.org/10.1023/A:1009886520142
19. Yu, Z., Klongthong, W., Thavorn, J., Ngamkroeckjoti, C.: Understanding rural Chinese consumers behavior: a stimulus–organism–response (SOR) perspective on Huawei's brand loyalty in China. Cogent. Bus. Manag. **8**(1), 1880679 (2021). https://doi.org/10.1080/23311975. 2021.1880679
20. Boyle, E.: A study of entrepreneurial brand building in the manufacturing sector in the UK. J. Prod. Brand Manage. **12**(2), 79–93 (2003). https://doi.org/10.1108/10610420310469779
21. O'Sullivan, D., Lim, K., Luck, J., Kenyon, A.T., Richardson, M., Ng-Loy, W.L.: What is the value of a brand to a firm? In: Kenyon, A.T., Richardson, M., Ng-Loy, W.L. (eds.) The Law of Reputation and Brands in the Asia Pacific, pp. 3–22. Cambridge University Press, Cambridge (2012)
22. Park, C.W., Milberg, S., Lawson, R.: Evaluation of brand extensions: the role of product feature similarity and brand concept consistency. J. Consum. Res. **18**(2), 185–193 (1991). https://doi.org/10.1086/209251
23. Park, C.W., Jaworski, B.J., MacInnis, D.J.: Strategic brand concept-image management. J. Mark. **50**(4), 135–145 (1986). https://doi.org/10.1177/002224298605000401
24. Lafley, A.G., Martin, R.L.: Playing to Win: how Strategy Really Works. Harvard Business Press, Boston (2013)
25. Stengel, J.R., Dixon, A.L., Allen, C.T.: Listening begins at home. Harv. Bus. Rev. **81**(11), 106–117 (2003)
26. Schultz, H.: Pour your Heart into it: How Starbucks Built a Company One Cup at a Time. Hyperion, New York (1997)
27. Dyson, J.: Against the Odds: an Autobiography. Texere, New York (2000)
28. Campbell, M.C., Keller, K.L.: Brand familiarity and advertising repetition effects. J. Consum. Res. **30**(2), 292–304 (2003). https://doi.org/10.1086/376800
29. Hoeffler, S., Keller, K.L.: The marketing advantages of strong brands. J. Brand Manag. **10**(6), 421–445 (2003). https://doi.org/10.1057/palgrave.bm.2540139
30. Zenker, S.: Measuring place brand equity with the advanced brand concept map (aBCM) method. Place Brand Public. Dipl. **10**(2), 158–166 (2014). https://doi.org/10.1057/pb.2014.2
31. Simões, C., Dibb, S.: Rethinking the brand concept: new brand orientation. Corp. Commun. **6**(4), 217–224 (2001). https://doi.org/10.1108/13563280110409854

32. Tilley, C.: Built-in branding: how to engineer a leadership brand. J. Mark. Manag. **15**(1–3), 181–191 (1999). https://doi.org/10.1362/026725799784870405
33. Gardner, B.B., Levy, S.J.: The product and the brand. Harv. Bus. Rev. **33**(2), 33–39 (1955)
34. Jin, L., Zou, D.: Extend to online or offline? The effects of web-brand extension mode, similarity, and brand concept on consumer evaluation. J. Mark. Manag. **29**(7–8), 755–771 (2013). https://doi.org/10.1080/0267257X.2013.796317
35. Lanseng, E., Olsen, L.E.: Brand alliances: the role of brand concept consistency. Eur. J. Mark. **46**(9), 1108–1126 (2012). https://doi.org/10.1108/03090561211247874
36. Punyatoya, P.: Evaluation of branding strategies for global versus local brand: the role of concept consistency. Int. J. Bus. Excell. **7**(1), 112–128 (2014). https://doi.org/10.1504/IJBEX.2014.057876
37. Thorbjørnsen, H.: Brand extensions: Brand concept congruency and feedback effects revisited. J. Prod. Brand Manag. **14**(4), 250–257 (2005). https://doi.org/10.1108/10610420510609258
38. Samuelsen, B.M., Olsen, L.E., Keller, K.L.: The multiple roles of fit between brand alliance partners in alliance attitude formation. Mark. Lett. **26**(4), 619–629 (2014). https://doi.org/10.1007/s11002-014-9297-y
39. Breitling (n.d.) Breitling × Bentley. Breitling. https://www.breitling.com/us-en/partnerships/breitling-and-bentley/
40. John, D.R., Loken, B., Kim, K., Monga, A.B.: Brand concept maps: a methodology for identifying brand association networks. J. Mark. Res. **43**(4), 549–563 (2006). https://doi.org/10.1509/jmkr.43.4.549
41. Schnittka, O., Sattler, H., Zenker, S.: Advanced brand concept maps: a new approach for evaluating the favorability of brand association networks. Int. J. Res. Mark. **29**(3), 265–274 (2012). https://doi.org/10.1016/j.ijresmar.2012.04.002
42. Hagtvedt, H., Patrick, V.M.: The broad embrace of luxury: hedonic potential as a driver of brand extendibility. J. Consum. Psychol. **19**(4), 608–618 (2009). https://doi.org/10.1016/j.jcps.2009.05.007
43. Topaloglu, O., Gokalp, O.N.: How brand concept affects consumer response to product recalls: a longitudinal study in the U.S. auto industry. J. Bus. Res. **88**, 245–254 (2018). https://doi.org/10.1016/j.jbusres.2018.03.035
44. Blount, S., Leinwand, P.: Why are we here? Harv. Bus. Rev. **97**(6), 132–139 (2019)
45. Kato, T.: Contribution of concept recall to brand loyalty: an empirical analysis of design and performance. J. Consum. Behav. 1–10 (2021). https://doi.org/10.1002/cb.1983
46. Joziasse, F.: Corporate strategy: bringing design management into the fold. Des. Manag. J. **11**(4), 36–41 (2000). https://doi.org/10.1111/j.1948-7169.2000.tb00146.x
47. Hollis, N. (eds.) Clarity of purpose. Brand Premium, Palgrave Macmillan, New York, pp. 71–82 (2013). https://doi.org/10.1007/978-1-137-51038-9_5
48. Lowe, B., Alpert, F.: Forecasting consumer perception of innovativeness. Technovation **45–46**, 1–14 (2015). https://doi.org/10.1016/j.technovation.2015.02.001

Pixel Importance: The Impact of Saturation and Brightness on the Spread of Information on Social Media

Timothy Kaskela[✉], Bin Zhu, and Sayali Dhamapurkar

Oregon State University, Corvallis, OR 97331, USA
`timothy.kaskela@oregonstate.edu`

Abstract. Social media engagement has been extensively studied, but there is an opportunity for greater understanding of how content embedded as an image or video may encourage certain behavior on social media. A pilot study is conducted to examine the effect of pixel level complexity measurements of saturation and brightness on the sharing behavior of individuals. The findings encourage a full study and will include an experimental study to use a multimethod approach for strengthening the final findings.

Keywords: Social media · Image complexity · Saturation · Brightness · Information spread

1 Introduction

Social media has become a vital communication avenue between a corporation and a consumer. With an estimated 233 million users of social media in the United States alone [7], it allows direct communication of a business's interests to a widespread audience. Social media has been found to affect brand reputation [13], impact firm value [19], and can even help to decrease the impact of negative online sentiment [12]. The nature of social media allows for a variety of engagement between an individual and a corporation, engagement can be via responses in the form of comments, through sharing behavior, or through passive consumption [5].

While the social media research field has been examined through many disciplines, there are still areas of opportunity for understanding the interactions that occur between an individual and a corporation, specifically how a corporate post would spread through a social media platform. The examination of the textual content of social media posts has been extensively studied [2], but there is an important component of a social media post that also needs to be considered – the media embedded within a social media post. The increase in the inclusion of an image or video within a social media post has led to a number of studies examining the impact of images in an online context [18, 22]. However, there is opportunity in the unstructured data of an image or video to extract further knowledge of how it impacts user behavior in a social media setting. This study examines how the visual elements of a social media post, specifically, the brightness and

S. Fan et al. (Eds.): WeB 2021, LNBIP 443, pp. 87–98, 2022.
https://doi.org/10.1007/978-3-031-04126-6_8

saturation of an image or video, affects how information spreads through a social media network. This leads to our research questions: How does media complexity in an online setting affect the spread of information from a corporate account?

The paper continues in the following manner: first, the theoretical foundation will be introduced and discussed. Second, hypothesis development will be conducted. Third, the methodology used to conduct a pilot study will be provided. Then, the results of the pilot study and planned future studies will be discussed. Post hoc analysis is then conducted and discussed to examine further variables that were not included in the initial analysis. Finally, the implication of the results will be explored.

2 Theoretical Background and Hypothesis Development

2.1 Social Media

The importance of social media research has led to numerous studies related to the behavior at both the individual and the corporate engagement perspective [20, 24]. When considering social media interactions between a corporation and the individual consumer, there have been studies that examined the impact of improvised marketing on virality and brand value [3] and the impact of corporate social media posts on financial returns [4]. The practical implications of creating positive customer engagements lends to the importance of understanding the drivers of that behavior. To that end, it has been posited that there are three distinctive types of social media engagement behaviors (SMEB) [6]. These three levels of engagement behavior are creating, contributing, and consuming. Behavior that creates content on a social media post, in response to a corporation, would include commenting on a post and is deemed active behavior. The second type of engagement is also considered active and would be for an individual to share a social media post. Lastly, the consumption social media engagement behavior is consuming the content without actively commenting, liking, or sharing it – this is considered to be passive SMEB. This study will focus on the SMEB of contribution and how it leads to sharing of social media posts.

2.2 Impact of Image

The increased usage of media embedded in a social media post has led to additional challenges to understanding engagement of social media posts versus posts consisting of only text. This shift in importance of image processing and customer engagement has led to recent studies that have examined the role of images within social media. Studies have examined how images within social media can be utilized to extract brand image [18], the impact of text and image complexity on reblogs and likes [22], and image characteristics, such as the presence of a human face and image quality [17]. Another important image characteristic is its complexity. The complexity of media has been considered through two different levels: object level and pixel level [22]. Three components of an image that can be measured at the pixel level includes the hue (color), value (brightness), and chroma (saturation) [8]. Research found that the emotional impact of an image is affected by all three components. The hue of an image has long been found to elicit different feelings of pleasure within an individual [10], additionally there has been some research related to the connection of the hue, brightness, and saturation to emotional elicitation [9, 26]. It is important to note that prior research at the pixel level has primarily focused on a static image. However, with the availability, and widespread use of video, on social networking sites, it will be vital to take into consideration social media posts that have videos embedded within them. Therefore, we will be examining the saturation and brightness of two types of media – both images and video. While the presence of a video or image will be controlled within the analysis, we will refer to both images and video that are embedded within the social media post.

2.3 Hypothesis Development

Prior research has found that emotional arousal has been linked to social transmission of information in an offline setting [2]. Additionally, the elicitation of positive emotions in an online setting also leads to increased sharing behavior [25]. Given the link between saturation and brightness and emotional response to an image, there is an opportunity to examine the effect of saturation and brightness of images and video on the social media engagement behavior of contribution via sharing a social media post. This paper will examine the contribution social media engagement behavior in which the individual who views a corporate social media post shares it, thus spreading the information embedded. Higher levels of brightness have been found to increase the feelings of relaxation and attitude, while it does not increase the feeling of excitement [9]. Brightness has also been found to increase feelings of pleasure [26]. The increased attitude and feelings of pleasure towards a social media post that has higher levels of brightness would be expected to increase the propensity of the individual to share the social media post. This leads us to our first hypothesis:

H1: A higher level of brightness in an image or video will increase the number of shares of a social media post.

Higher levels of saturation have been found to increase excitement and attitude towards an image [9], as well as pleasure [26]. As the reaction has been found to be similar for the emotional reactions for both brightness and saturation, we expect that the response will be similar. This increased emotional response to saturation would be expected to lead to the social transmission of information. Therefore, we would expect that a higher saturation of an image will increase the sharing of a social media post, leading us to our second hypothesis:

H2: A higher level of saturation in an image or video will increase the number of shares of a social media post.

The research model for the study is presented in Fig. 1:

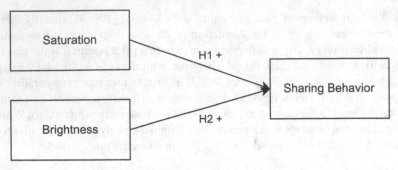

Fig. 1. Research model

3   Method

A pilot study was conducted using Twitter, due to the 206 million monetizable daily active users and the prevalence of companies using the platform [23]. One year of tweets were collected from a single corporate Twitter account (Samsung Mobile). All tweets that were in response to other users were removed to focus on original content created by the corporation. The final dataset included a total number of 439 tweets from the corporation. The dependent variable focuses on the sharing of information and counts the number of shares of a tweet by the selected corporation, measured through the retweet feature on Twitter. The average number of retweets ranged from 4 to 117,582, with a mean of 8,839.

Following prior social media studies, media type, the time of day, the day of the week, and the inclusion of a celebrity endorser were included as control variables [3, 11, 14, 17]. The time of day was found by putting the posts into 6 h bins, starting at midnight, Eastern Standard Time. A key component of an image that impacts emotional response has been found to be the hue (colors) included within the image [26], therefore the red, green, and blue hues were also included as control variables. The predominant hue of the three primary hues were added as the control. The independent variables were the media complexity variables of saturation and brightness.

To measure the two independent variables in an image and the hue control variable, each image was converted to a matrix of pixels the same length and width of the image. Each element within the matrix contained three values, the hue, saturation, and brightness of the pixel it represented in the image. Python was utilized to calculate the hue, saturation, and brightness, of each pixel contained within an image, then the average of the entire image was calculated.

As previously mentioned, it is possible to also embed videos within a tweet. Therefore, a control variable was included for the media type, as well as a calculation for the media variables (hue, brightness, and saturation). For a video, each frame of the video was extracted as an image. Then, the same method was used to calculate the hue, brightness, and saturation variables. The final variable value for each video was the average of the average pixels across the entire video for all three complexity measurements. Brightness ranged from 0 to 255 and had a mean of 143.54. The saturation of the image was on a scale from 0 to 1 and had an average of 0.17. Interestingly, there was an image with saturation of 0.00, indicating a white image. The first time block is from 12 a.m. to 6 a.m. (EST for all times) and had a mean of 0.11, meaning 11% of the tweets were posted between 12 a.m. and 6 a.m. This would be expected, since it would be expected that most tweets are posted when social media usage would be increased, not at such an early time of day. The second time block is from 6 a.m. to 12 p.m. and has a mean of 0.16. The third time block is from 12 p.m. to 6 p.m. and has a mean of 0.67, which would be the expected time block for the majority of the tweets to be posted. The fourth time block is from 6 p.m. to 12 a.m. and has a mean of 0.06. The weekend control had a mean of 0.17, meaning 17% of the posts were posted on the weekend. The red hue control is a binary variable with a mean of 0.32, meaning 32% of the posts were primarily with a red hue. The green hue control is a binary variable with a mean of 0.52, meaning 52% of the posts had a green hue. Finally, the blue hue variable was 0.16, representing 16% of the dataset. The media type variable has an average of 0.84, meaning that 84% of the tweets had a video. An antecedent of positive emotion elicitation has been found to be the inclusion of a celebrity endorser [25], therefore a control variable is included when a celebrity is included in the media or the text of the tweet. 19% of the tweets included an endorser, which was typically the band BTS. The sentiment of the tweet was calculated using Python and vaderSentiment from the nltk package [15]. The sentiment is calculated on a range from -1 to $+1$. The sentiment of the corporate tweet had a mean of 0.25. It would be expected that most of the tweets would have a positive sentiment, which results in the positive mean. However, with a range from -0.62 to 0.98, there were some tweets that had negative. The summary statistics for the 439 social media posts are included in Table 1.

Table 1. Summary statistics

Measures	M	SD	Minimum	Maximum
Dependent measure				
Retweet count	8,838.50	21,377.98	4.00	117,582.00
Media measures				
Brightness	143.54	59.36	10.75	254.70
Saturation	0.17	0.13	0.00	0.72
Control measures				
Posted between 0:01 to 12:00	0.11	0.31	0.00	1.00
Posted between 06:00 to 12:00	0.16	0.36	0.00	1.00
Posted between 12:00 to 18:00	0.67	0.47	0.00	1.00
Posted between 18:00 to 24:00	0.06	0.24	0.00	1.00
Weekend	0.17	0.38	0.00	1.00
Red hue	0.32	0.47	0.00	1.00
Green hue	0.52	0.50	0.00	1.00
Blue hue	0.16	0.37	0.00	1.00
Media type (0 = image, 1 = video)	0.84	0.37	0.00	1.00
Celebrity endorser (0 or 1)	0.19	0.39	0.00	1.00
Corporate tweet sentiment (-1 to 1)	0.25	0.35	-0.62	0.98

4 Results

As the number of retweets followed a Poisson distribution, a generalized linear model was estimated with the assumption of a Poisson distribution. To examine the significance of the independent variables, first a model was estimated with only the control variables. A second model with the direct effects of the selected independent variables was then estimated. The research model is as follows:

$$Retweets_p = \beta_0 + \beta_1 TimeofDay_p + \beta_2 HueBin_p$$
$$+ \beta_3 CorporateTweetSentiment_p + \beta_4 Weekend_p + \beta_5 MediaType_p$$
$$+ \beta_6 CelebrityEndorser_p + \beta_7 Brightness_p + \beta_8 Saturation_p + \varepsilon_p \qquad (1)$$

Where p is the respective post. As the Time of Day and Hue Bin variables are categorical, they each have reference levels. The reference level for the time of day is from midnight to 6 a.m. (00:00 to 06:00) and the reference level for the hue is the red hue. The corporate tweet sentiment controls for the sentiment of the text of the initial tweet. The weekend variable is a binary variable that is zero for weekdays and one for weekends. The media type variable is either an image or video, the reference level is that of an image. The celebrity endorser variable is a dummy variable and controls for the inclusion of a reference to a celebrity in the image, video, or tweet of the text. The significance of the increase in the AIC between the models was then tested. The difference between the two models was highly statistically significant ($p < 0.001$), meaning that the addition of the brightness and saturation variables improved the estimation of the retweets in a significant manner. The results of the pilot study found are presented in Table 2.

Table 2. Model results table

Variable	Model 1		Model 2	
Intercept	6.952***	(0.003)	6.634***	(0.003)
Controls				
Posted between 06:00 to 12:00	−0.108***	(0.002)	0.066***	(0.002)
Posted between 12:00 to 18:00	−0.301***	(0.002)	−0.200***	(0.002)
Posted between 18:00 to 24:00	−0.047***	(0.003)	0.236***	(0.003)
Green hue	0.045***	(0.002)	0.291***	(0.002)
Blue hue	0.573***	(0.002)	0.582***	(0.002)
Corporate tweet sentiment	−0.217***	(0.002)	−0.121***	(0.002)
Weekend	−0.109***	(0.002)	−0.292***	(0.002)
Media type	0.123***	(0.001)	0.145***	(0.001)
Celebrity endorser	1.826***	(0.001)	1.788***	(0.001)
Main effects				
Brightness			−0.357***	(0.001)
Saturation			0.055***	(0.001)
AIC	1740347		1486468	
Difference between models			$p < 0.001$	

Model 1 included only the control variable. It showed a positive effect of a celebrity endorser (1.826, $p < 0.001$) and that the inclusion of a video had a significantly higher impact on sharing behavior than an image (0.123, $p < 0.001$). Tweets posted on the weekend had less shares than tweets posted on a weekday (-0.109, $p < 0.001$). Interestingly, the sentiment of a tweet had a negative impact on sharing behavior (-0.217, $p < 0.001$). Tweets with an image or video with a blue hue had the highest amount of share over the red and green hues (0.573, $p < 0.001$). Overall, the control model showed significant effects of the control variables on sharing behavior, as would be expected.

For the full model (Model 2), the control variables were found to be significant in terms of the time of day in which the tweet was posted, the overriding color included within the embedded media, the sentiment of the text contained in the corporate tweet, whether the tweet was posted on a weekend, and if a celebrity endorser was included in the tweet. This was to be expected, as they have been found to be significant factors in prior studies on social media engagement [3, 11, 14, 17]. The main effects also both had significant effects on the number of retweets of a corporate social media post. The brightness of the image was significant (-0.357, $p < 0.001$), but interestingly suggested that an image that is brighter reduces the number of retweets, not supporting H1. The saturation of the image was significantly positive (0.055, $p < 0.001$), suggesting that the inclusion of more saturation in an image will increase the information spread through a social media network, supporting H2.

It may be possible that the emotions that elicit information sharing react differently to brightness and saturation. Feelings of pleasure were found to be elicited by increased saturation and increased brightness. However, arousal was previously found to be negatively affected by brightness and positively affected by saturation. The link between emotion and information sharing may be primarily associated with arousal over pleasure. The negative impact of brightness on retweets and the positive impact of saturation may be explained through that link [26]. To assess the results of the pilot study, a full study will be conducted, as well as two experiments. The experiments will help to determine the impact of the emotional impact of saturation and brightness on information sharing.

4.1 Future Studies

A subsequent study on Twitter will be conducted collecting data from a total of 30 companies encompassing the Dow Jones Industrial Average index. This will increase the generalizability of the results and expand the dataset to be collected for the final analysis. Additionally, variables that were not included in the pilot study will also be included. The post content of the corporation (Samsung) was similar in the pilot study, but greater understanding of the sharing behavior would be strengthened by classifying the different types of posts. The complexity of the images utilized in the social media posts will be calculated as a control variable. The additional study will also control for the strong impact of the celebrity endorser that was present in the pilot study.

The unexpected negative impact of brightness on the sharing behavior on social media is something that will be further examined. It may be that there is an interaction effect of brightness and saturation that will need to be further examined. A potential u-shape or inverse u-shape of both saturation and brightness will also be examined in the full study on Twitter and through experiments.

To strengthen the results of the pilot study and the subsequent full study, experimental studies are also planned with manipulation of the saturation and brightness in an image that will be presented to the participant is a mock social media setting. The first experiment is positioned to isolate the emotional response to saturation, as well as the sharing behavior based on saturation. After isolating the impact of saturation, the interaction of brightness and saturation will also be examined in a second experiment. This will ensure that the findings of the pilot study, and subsequent study conducted on Twitter, will be strengthened with a multimethod approach, and will examine the relationship between saturation and brightness in media on social media.

5 Post Hoc Analysis

Post hoc analysis was conducted to expand on the pilot study research model. Four additional control variables were added to the pilot model to control for further unexamined effects. The pilot study examines the average brightness and average saturation of the full image or video. However, the difference of the brightness and saturation across the media type utilized may also influence sharing behavior. Therefore, the standard deviation of brightness and saturation was included in the post hoc model as a proxy measurement of the amount of contrast within the media type. The number of followers on a monthly basis for Samsung Mobile during 2020 was included in the post hoc model as well to control any increased sharing behavior that may have occurred based upon the number of followers of the corporate account at the time of the tweet. The interaction between saturation and brightness has been established in previous research [26] and will be included in the post hoc analysis as well. With the added variables the model examined in the post hoc analysis is the following:

$$
\begin{aligned}
Retweets_p = {} & \beta_0 + \beta_1 TimeofDay_p + \beta_2 HueBin_p \\
& + \beta_3 CorporateTweetSentiment_p + \beta_4 Weekend_p + \beta_5 MediaType_p \\
& + \beta_6 CelebrityEndorser_p + \beta_7 Followers + \beta_8 HueStdDev + \beta_9 SatStdDev \\
& + \beta_{10} BrightStdDev + \beta_{11} Brightness_p + \beta_{12} Saturation_p + \beta_{13} Brightness \\
& * Saturation + \varepsilon_p
\end{aligned}
\tag{2}
$$

Again, where p denotes the social media post (tweet). The additional variables are the number of followers that are standardized, the standard deviation of the hue as a proxy as the change in the colors of the media type, the standard deviation of the saturation and standard deviation of the saturation are also included to control for changes in the brightness and saturation across the media type. The interaction between saturation and brightness was also included to examine any potential relationship between the two variables. The difference between the pilot study model and the post hoc model were found to be significantly different ($p < 0.001$) (Table 3).

The post hoc model found a significant effect of the time of day in which a tweet is posted. Again, as the time of day is a categorical variable, it has a reference level of tweets posted between 0:00 and 6:00. The reference level for the hue is again the red hue. The green (0.164, $p < 0.001$) and blue hue (0.305, p < 0.001) both had a significantly higher effect on the number of retweets than the red hue, similar to the pilot

Table 3. Post hoc model

Variable	Model	
Intercept	7.251***	(0.005)
Controls		
Posted between 06:00 to 12:00	−0.036***	(0.002)
Posted between 12:00 to 18:00	−0.209***	(0.002)
Posted between 18:00 to 24:00	0.346***	(0.003)
Green hue	0.164***	(0.003)
Blue hue	0.305***	(0.003)
Corporate tweet sentiment	−0.132***	(0.002)
Weekend	−0.382***	(0.002)
Media type	0.052***	(0.001)
Celebrity endorser	1.781***	(0.001)
Number of followers	0.108***	(0.001)
Hue standard deviation	0.688***	(0.009)
Saturation standard deviation	−1.938***	(0.018)
Brightness standard deviation	−1.238***	(0.011)
Main effects		
Brightness	−0.337***	(0.001)
Saturation	0.083***	(0.001)
Interaction effect		
Brightness * Saturation	−0.070***	(0.001)
AIC	1395377	
Difference between models	$p < 0.001$	

study model. Additionally, the corporate sentiment of the tweet ($-0.132, p < 0.001$) and tweets posted on the weekend ($-0.382, p < 0.001$) both had a negative impact on the number of retweets. Media type ($0.052, p < 0.001$) had a positive significant effect, meaning that tweets that had a video had a significantly higher number of shares than posts with an image, holding all other effects equal. The celebrity endorser, similar to the pilot study model, has a strong impact on the number of retweets ($1.781, p < 0.001$).

Of the new control variables included in the model, the number of followers had a positive impact on the number of retweets ($0.108, p < 0.001$). This makes sense as a higher number of followers would mean a larger number of individuals saw the tweet, which could lead to more retweets. The standard deviation of the hues was found to have a positive, significant impact on the number of retweets ($0.688, p < 0.001$), which would suggest that the inclusion of more colors would lead to a larger number of retweets. The standard deviation of both saturation ($-1.938, p < 0.001$) and brightness (-1.238,

$p < 0.001$) are both negative. This would suggest that consistency of saturation and brightness will lead to a greater number of retweets.

The interaction between brightness and saturation was also found to be significant (-0.070, $p < 0.001$) and negative. This suggests that there is a negative relationship between saturation and brightness in regards to sharing behavior. As the direct effect of brightness is found to be negative and the direct effect of saturation is found to be positive, this would suggest that the highest number of retweets, in terms of the examined variables, can be attained with higher saturation and lower brightness.

The link between saturation and brightness has been found to impact the arousal of various emotions [9, 26]. Emotional arousal has been found to impact information transmission and sharing in both offline and online settings [2, 25]. Our pilot study and post hoc analysis attempts to establish a link on the impact of saturation and brightness on information sharing. The experimental studies that are planned will strive to connect saturation and brightness with information sharing via emotional arousal.

6 Discussion

The explosive growth in users of various social media platforms has led to a unique opportunity for a corporation to leverage engagement with the individual consumer in an unprecedented manner. Engagement between the individual and corporation has been shown to have a positive impact of sentiment and receptivity [16], customer visits [21], and improve shareholder value when done correctly [1]. Another potential avenue through which social media platforms can be leveraged is by encouraging the spread of information that is sourced from a corporation. The drivers of such sharing behavior have grown in importance, leading to a more nuanced understanding of how to elicit such behavior. Prior research has found that emotional arousal leads to information transmission in an offline setting [2]. Additionally, saturation and brightness have been found to impact emotional arousal. Our pilot study connects a link between saturation and brightness with information sharing. Subsequent planned studies will further examine the link and establish how saturation and brightness effect the sharing behavior on a social media platform. By isolating the impact of certain complexity features of media, it furthers the understanding of the impact of media complexity on sharing behavior.

Building on the understanding of arousal and information sharing, this pilot study lends to that literature by introducing two pixel level measurements that could lead to more sharing of a social media post. Further development of the pilot study into a full study, as well as the inclusion of experimental studies will allow for greater understanding of the impact of how the complexity of an image or video may lead to the desired customer engagement behavior from the consumer. This would have practical implications for social media managers who could then leverage the findings to create social media posts that would encourage more sharing of the message that the corporation wishes to disseminate. Establishing the impact on brightness and saturation on emotional arousal, then establishing the impact of emotional arousal on sharing behavior will give greater understanding to the composition of an image or a video in order to share information through a network. Depending on the goal of the social media manager, the creation of the media to include within a tweet can lead to greater impact. This pilot study creates the foundation for the establishment of the impact of brightness and saturation on emotion and the subsequent impact on sharing behavior. Further research will work to strengthen the findings through a complete study on social media behavior and two experimental studies that will isolate the impact of both saturation and brightness.

References

1. Beckers, S.F.M., van Doorn, J., Verhoef, P.C.: Good, better, engaged? The effect of company-initiated customer engagement behavior on shareholder value. J. Acad. Mark. Sci. **46**(3), 366–383 (2017). https://doi.org/10.1007/s11747-017-0539-4
2. Berger, J.: Arousal Increases social transmission of information. Psychol. Sci. **22**(7), 891–893 (2011). https://doi.org/10.1177/0956797611413294
3. Borah, A., Banerjee, S., Lin, Y.T., Jain, A., Eisingerich, A.B.: Improvised marketing interventions in social media. J. Mark. **84**(2), 69–91 (2020). https://doi.org/10.1177/0022242919899383
4. Chung, S., Animesh, A., Han, K., Pinsonneault, A.: Financial returns to firms' communication actions on firm-initiated social media: evidence from Facebook business pages. Inf. Syst. Res. **31**(1), 258–285 (2020). https://doi.org/10.1287/isre.2019.0884
5. Dolan, R., Conduit, J., Fahy, J., Goodman, S.: Social media engagement behaviour: a uses and gratifications perspective. J. Strateg. Mark. **24**(3–4), 261–277 (2016)
6. Dolan, R., Frethey-Bentham, C., Fahy, J., Goodman, S.: Social media engagement behavior a framework for engaging customers through social media content. Eur. J. Mark. **53**(10), 2213–2243 (2019). https://doi.org/10.1108/EJM-03-2017-0182
7. Edison Research.: The Infinite Dial 2021 (2021)
8. Gorn, G.J., Chattopadhyay, A., Sengupta, J., Tripathi, S.: Waiting for the web: how screen color affects time perception. J. Mark. Res. **41**(2), 215–225 (2004). https://doi.org/10.1509/jmkr.41.2.215.28668
9. Gorn, G.J., Chattopadhyay, A., Yi, T., Dahl, D.W.: Effects of color as an executional cue in advertising: they're in the shade. Manage. Sci. **43**(10), 1387–1400 (1997). https://doi.org/10.1287/mnsc.43.10.1387
10. Guilford, A.J.P., Smith, P.C.: A system of color-preferences. Am. J. Psychol. **72**(4), 487–502 (1959)
11. Han, Y., Lappas, T., Sabnis, G.: The importance of interactions between content characteristics and creator characteristics for studying virality in social media. Inf. Syst. Res. **31**(2), 576–588 (2020). https://doi.org/10.1287/ISRE.2019.0903
12. Herhausen, D., Ludwig, S., Grewal, D., Wulf, J., Schoegel, M.: Detecting, preventing, and mitigating online firestorms in brand communities. J. Mark. **83**(3), 1–21 (2019). https://doi.org/10.1177/0022242918822300
13. Hewett, K., Rand, W., Rust, R.T., van Heerde, H.J.: Brand buzz in the echoverse. J. Mark. **80**(3), 1–24 (2016). https://doi.org/10.1509/jm.15.0033
14. Hughes, C., Swaminathan, V., Brooks, G.: Driving brand engagement through online social influencers: an empirical investigation of sponsored blogging campaigns. J. Mark. **83**(5), 78–96 (2019). https://doi.org/10.1177/0022242919854374
15. Hutto, C.J., Gilbert, E.: Vader: a parsimonious rule-based model for sentiment analysis of social media text. In: Eighth International AAAI Conference on Weblogs and Social Media, pp. 216–225 (2014)
16. Kumar, A., Bezawada, R., Rishika, R., Janakiraman, R., Kannan, P.K.: From social to sale: the effects of firm-generated content in social media on customer behavior. J. Mark. **80**(1), 7–25 (2016). https://doi.org/10.1509/jm.14.0249

17. Li, Y., Xie, Y.: Is a picture worth a thousand words? An empirical study of image content and social media engagement. J. Mark. Res. **57**(1), 1–19 (2020). https://doi.org/10.1177/002224 3719881113
18. Liu, L., Dzyabura, D., Mizik, N.: Visual listening in: extracting brand image portrayed on social media. Mark. Sci. **39**(4), 669–686 (2020). https://doi.org/10.1287/mksc.2020.1226
19. Nguyen, H., Calantone, R., Krishnan, R.: Influence of social media emotional word of mouth on institutional investors' decisions and firm value. Manage. Sci. **66**(2), 887–910 (2020). https://doi.org/10.1287/mnsc.2018.3226
20. Qiu, L., Tang, Q., Whinston, A.B.: Two formulas for success in social media: learning and network effects. J. Manag. Inf. Syst. **32**(4), 78–108 (2015). https://doi.org/10.1080/07421222. 2015.1138368
21. Rishika, R., Kumar, A., Janakiraman, R., Bezawada, R.: The effect of customers' social media participation on customer visit frequency and profitability: an empirical investigation. Inf. Syst. Res. **24**(1), 108–127 (2013)
22. Shin, D., He, S., Lee, G.M., Whinston, A.B., Cetintas, S., Lee, K.-C.: Enhancing social media analysis with visual analytics: a deep learning approach. MIS Q. **44**(4), 1459–1492 (2020). https://doi.org/10.2139/ssrn.2830377
23. Statista.: Twitter global mDAU 2021, Statista. https://www.statista.com/statistics/970920/ monetizable-daily-active-twitter-users-worldwide/
24. Susarla, A., Oh, J.H., Tan, Y.: Influentials, imitables, or susceptibles? Virality and word-of-mouth conversations in online social networks. J. Manag. Inf. Syst. **33**(1), 139–170 (2016). https://doi.org/10.1080/07421222.2016.1172454
25. Tellis, G.J., MacInnis, D.J., Tirunillai, S., Zhang, Y.: What drives virality (Sharing) of online digital content? The critical role of information, emotion, and brand prominence. J. Mark. **83**(4), 1–20 (2019). https://doi.org/10.1177/0022242919841034
26. Valdez, P., Mehrabian, A.: Effects of color on emotions. J. Exp. Psychol. Gen. **123**(4), 394–409 (1994). https://doi.org/10.1037/0096-3445.123.4.394

Author Index

Printed in the United States
by Baker & Taylor Publisher Services